52 WEEKLY DEVOTIONALS
FROM
EVERYDAY TRUTH

Once a week, go deeper with God.

From the blog at AdventuresinChristianity.net

By Casey Hawley

ISBN: 9781700340023

About the Cover

Why is the fence the image for the cover of this book and for the blog from AdventuresinChristianity.net entitled *Everyday Truth*? Because Casey simply shares the unvarnished truths from God's Word and from decades of walking with Him and seeing how He operates. In the South, there is a saying that something is as "plain as a fencepost." God's ways need no adornment or exaggerated claims, and Casey seeks to make plain those eternal truths. They are "everyday truths" to all who have come to believe in God.

About the Book

Be introduced to a God who is full of surprises, full of Grace, and full of power that He longs to put to use in your life. This God of unexpected twists and turns makes living life with Him a nonstop adventure because He is the God with the capital "G" that you may have been been wondering about. Whether you want to know Him more intimately or just want to know Him at all, **Everyday Truth** will help you spend time with Him once a week in a way that is deeper, more meaningful, and richer than the typical daily devotional book. If you are looking for more, then prayerfully consider adding this book once a week to your pursuit of God.

The book offers 52 devotionals, one for each week of the year, to bring you into a deeper relationship with the Lord. The devotionals deal with the trials and joys we all face and give you the God-perspective on each one. Seasons and holidays are the special focus of some of the readings to prepare your heart and keep Him at the center of those busy times. Every calendar year is different, but those special devotionals occur in close proximity to the dates of each holiday. Packed with Scripture and brief stories of God at work in real lives, the devotions give you glimpses of God every week so you can understand His ways better and begin to know authentically who the God of the universe really is. The devotionals were originally blog posts from Casey's website, AdventuresinChristianity.net.

52 WEEKLY DEVOTIONALS FROM
EVERYDAY TRUTH

ONCE A WEEK, GO DEEPER WITH GOD

DEVOTIONAL 1: STONES OF REMEMBRANCE

Might God be doing a new thing in your heart in this year? Are you open to it? Eager for it? A bit afraid of what it might mean? Consider whether setting up a stone of remembrance might be a good way for you to begin your year with your dear Father. Let me explain what I mean by a stone of remembrance.

We don't have to give God gifts. He certainly does not need anything from us since He is the owner and supplier of everything. But in this recent season of my life, I have discovered the joy of giving a gift just because. It is similar to how wonderful a wife feels when her husband surprises her with a gift just to say, "I love you," when there is no expectation as there might be on an anniversary or birthday.

My favorite kind of spontaneous "I love you" gift is patterned after the stones of remembrance that so many great leaders from the Old Testament established when God blessed them or rescued them. The first stone of remembrance gift I can remember giving was when I sat down to write a sort of journal to the Lord. Every day, I sat and acknowledged to Him something He had delivered me from in my life. I had realized I had never stopped to say, "I get it. You did this. I did not get out of that pit by myself." Although those journal entries became my book **Adventures in Christianity**, originally, it was just a private thank you between the Lord and me.

In 2017, one of Atlanta's most historic black churches, Friendship Baptist, sold their prime Atlanta property in order for the Falcons to build their new stadium. The story of how this church was established in 1856 is a story of setting up a stone of remembrance. Remember that in those days, the voyage from Africa was one many enslaved men and women did not survive. A group of slaves who had recently come to Atlanta made establishing their own church a priority. The impoverished congregation met in a discarded boxcar for years, but they never stopped praying about and saving to establish a place of worship, God's house. Their sacrifice in setting up their own church was a testimony to God. In looking at our own circumstances of the last year, we can learn much from these people after God's heart.

I recently had prayed for a friend's husband to get a job. When he got the job, my heart was prompted to acknowledge that this was from God's hand, so I made a small donation to Leading the Way as a stone of remembrance. I don't do that for every person who gets a job I pray for, but I was prompted to do it in that instance. That is the key. We don't establish these stones as ritual, habit, or requirements. Some people burst into song at the goodness of the Lord and some write poems, but those things may not be your style. Anyone can establish a stone of remembrance. Just very intentionally set aside time to acknowledge something He has done that you reverence or appreciate, or it can be a tribute to one of His character traits you are in awe of. Your stone may be that you set aside an hour or a day for Him. If you are an artist, depict your gratitude through a painting or sketch or sculpture. Whatever gratitude is flowing out of you, use it to express to Him that you know He is the giver of all good things, and that without Him, no good thing exists. If art is not your thing, give of your unique gifts—hospitality, giving, or anything you feel your heart moved to do to honor Him. Just remember this caveat: the stone of remembrance is not required, but is a loving response from your heart.

This month we will study some unforgettable people who accomplished amazing things and left their imprint on not just Christianity but on the history of the world. All had at least one moment when they stopped and set up stones of remembrance to acknowledge that they did not deserve the credit but that God did it all, only using them to accomplish His purpose.

To prepare your heart for next week's post, read Joshua 4 from the Bible. Prayerfully ask God what He is saying to you through these verses. Is your heart prompted to respond to Him in a new way in the coming year?

Joshua 4

*When all the nation had finished passing over the Jordan, the Lord said to Joshua, **2** "Take twelve men from the people, from each tribe a man, **3** and command them, saying, 'Take twelve stones from here out of the midst of the Jordan, from the very place where the priests' feet stood firmly, and bring them over with you and lay them down in the place where you lodge tonight.'" **4** Then Joshua called the twelve men from the people of Israel, whom he had appointed, a man from each* tribe. *5 And Joshua said to them, "Pass on before the ark of the Lord your God into the midst of the Jordan, and take up each of you a stone upon his shoulder, according to the number of the tribes of the people of Israel, 6 that this may be a sign among you. When your children ask in time to come, 'What do those stones mean to you?' 7 then you shall tell them that the waters of the Jordan were cut off before the ark of the covenant of the Lord. When it passed over the Jordan, the waters of the Jordan were cut off. So these stones shall be to the people of Israel a memorial forever."*

8 And the people of Israel did just as Joshua commanded and took up twelve stones out of the midst of the Jordan, according to the number of the tribes of the people of Israel, just as the Lord told Joshua. And they carried them over with them to the place where they lodged and laid them down[a] there. 9 And Joshua set up[b] twelve stones in the midst of the Jordan, in the place where the feet of the priests bearing the ark of the covenant had stood; and they are there to this day. 10 For the priests bearing the ark stood in the midst of the Jordan until everything was finished that the Lord commanded Joshua to tell the people, according to all that Moses had commanded Joshua. The people passed over in haste. 11 And when all the people had finished passing over, the ark of the Lord and the priests passed over before the people. 12 The sons of Reuben and the sons of Gad and the half-tribe of Manasseh passed over armed before the people of Israel, as Moses had told them. 13 About 40,000 ready for war passed over before the Lord for battle, to the plains of Jericho. 14 On that day the Lord exalted Joshua in the sight of all Israel, and they stood in awe of him just as they had stood in awe of Moses, all the days of his life. 15 And the Lord said to Joshua, 16 "Command the priests bearing the ark of the testimony to come up out of the Jordan." 17 So Joshua commanded the priests, "Come up out of the Jordan." 18 And when the priests bearing the ark of the covenant of the Lord came up from the midst of the Jordan, and the soles of the priests' feet were lifted up on dry ground, the waters of the Jordan returned to their place and overflowed all its banks, as before.

19 The people came up out of the Jordan on the tenth day of the first month, and they encamped at Gilgal on the east border of Jericho. 20 And those twelve stones, which they took out of the Jordan, Joshua set up at Gilgal. 21 And he said to the people of Israel, "When *your children ask their fathers in times to come, 'What do these stones mean?' **22** then you shall let your children know, 'Israel passed over this Jordan on dry ground.' **23** For the Lord your God dried up the waters of the Jordan for you until you passed over, as the Lord your God did to the Red Sea, which he dried up for us until we passed over, **24** so that all the peoples of the earth may know that the hand of the Lord is mighty, that you may fear the Lord your God forever."*

DEVOTIONAL 2: HOW TO RESPOND TO SUCCESS

To say that Joshua had been through some hard times with Moses and the Israelites in their journey to the Promised Land would be a huge understatement. He had put in decades of hard work, risked his life too many times to count, and faced opposition from enemies even within his own circle of friends and family (Unfamiliar with the story? Read the book of Exodus and then Joshua 1-4. If you do not have a Bible, you can Google this adventure story.) When the day finally came that Joshua and the people of God could cross the Jordan River and enter the wonderful land their fathers had been promised so long ago, it was an overpoweringly momentous occasion. Most men who had led a difficult mission like this would have been thinking of all they had done and that their sacrifices were at last paying off. But Joshua was not boasting of his accomplishment. He was still listening to God. Just as God had told him what to do in his struggles and battles, God was telling Him what to do in his victory and rest. Have you ever thought about your response in the seasons of victory and rest? Are you in such a season now? Are you prepared for success when it comes?

Visualize this scene as the multitude of people at long last cross over the river to their destination and the last Israelite sets foot on dry land:

*"When all the nation had finished passing over the Jordan, the Lord said to Joshua, **2** "Take twelve men from the people, from each tribe a man, **3** and command them, saying, 'Take twelve stones from here out of the midst of the Jordan, from the very place where the priests' feet stood firmly, and bring them over with you and lay them down in the place where you lodge tonight.'" ... When your children ask in time to come, 'What do those stones mean to you?' **7** then you shall tell them that the waters of the Jordan were cut off before the ark of the covenant of the Lord. When it passed over the Jordan, the waters of the Jordan were cut off. So these stones shall be to the people of Israel a memorial forever.' " Joshua 4:1-2, 6b-7.*

After an arduous journey like that and a full out effort to be a part of God's purpose, I fear I would be tempted to say, "Really, Lord? Today? Can't we just celebrate here for the day? Can't we just sit here on the riverbank? I feel I have earned a bit of a rest. Don't get me wrong, Lord, I will give you your due. But does it need to come first and at a time that is not best for me?"

Yes, it needs to come first. Giving the Lord His due always comes first. It is not His role to fit around our list of priorities, our schedules, and our waxing and waning energy levels. He comes first. And you don't notice any discussion of that or analyzing of that by Joshua. One thing I like about Joshua is that he is teachable. He listens to what God says should be his response to the successful crossing into the Promised Land. He starts to work instantly, and the enormous, heavy stones are moved. God chose the right man to lead His people into the Promised Land. Joshua had his priorities in the correct order, and honoring God was number one. Are you teachable? What is the Lord stirring in your heart this month?

How about your to-do list? Is honoring God number one?

... so that all the peoples of the earth may know that the hand of the Lord is mighty, that you may fear the Lord your God forever. Joshua 4:24

DEVOTIONAL 3: WHAT YOU CAN DO ABOUT THE FUTURE

Genesis 28:10-19

10 Jacob left Beersheba and set out for Harran. 11 When he reached a certain place, he stopped for the night because the sun had set. Taking one of the stones there, he put it under his head and lay down to sleep.12 He had a dream in which he saw a stairway resting on the earth, with its top reaching to heaven, and the angels of God were ascending and descending on it. 13 There above it stood the Lord, and he said: 'I am the Lord, the God of your father Abraham and the God of Isaac. I will give you and your descendants the land on which you are lying. 14 Your descendants will be like the dust of the earth, and you will spread out to the west and to the east, to the north and to the south. All peoples on earth will be blessed through you and your offspring. 15 I am with you and will watch over you wherever you go, and I will bring you back to this land. I will not leave you until I have done what I have promised you.'

16 When Jacob awoke from his sleep, he thought, "Surely the Lord is in this place, and I was not aware of it." 17 He was afraid and said, 'How awesome is this place! This is none other than the house of God; this is the gate of heaven.'

18 Early the next morning Jacob took the stone he had placed under his head and set it up as a pillar and poured oil on top of it. 19 He called that place Bethel, though the city used to be called Luz.

Jacob was a man who understood that his future was truly God's to do with as He saw fit. He understood that whatever had happened to him thus far and whatever was about to happen to him next was sifted through God's fingers. Knowing he was completely subject to the mercy of God prompted Jacob to communicate with the Lord and to acknowledge Him publicly.

On Jacob's journey back to the homeland of his grandfather Abraham, he stops to sleep at Bethel. In his dream, God tells Jacob that He will give him the land on which he is lying. Even more wonderful to a Jewish man of his time, he tells Jacob he will multiply his offspring and bless them. It is significant that God has already told Jacob this **before** Jacob sets up a pillar of remembrance. God has spoken and God cannot lie. It is a done deal.

Jacob is not trying to curry favor with God. God has already told him he is going to be favored in the most valuable ways a man could be blessed in his day—with land and descendants. Jacob's setting up the pillar is a recognition of what God has already done and there is no motive in it but to give God glory.

That is the second caveat when you are setting up a stone of remembrance. It cannot have hidden in it the hope that you will earn God's love or mercy. You already have that. If you understand your Father in Heaven, you know that nothing you can do for Him will increase His love and mercy. He has that in extravagant measure-beyond what we can fathom. He loves you as one loves any imperfect child, and we are all imperfect. He has gone to extreme measures to bless us despite our limited understanding of His love and His Grace. May we be like Jacob that our only response to His outpouring of love and promises to care for us is just to acknowledge Him and to honor Him with our nod to Him—whatever form that takes. It may be just a prayer that is a thank you for all that He has done for you thus far (and there is much He has done for you that you don't even know.) It may be a prayer that acknowledges that you cannot see the future, but that you trust Him and know He will be taking care of you and guiding you from this point forward. Give Him the honor of trusting Him today, even if you cannot fully understand all the events and circumstances of your life so far. Your life's journey may have been a rocky one, and people and events may make you feel insecure. But He is the secure place you can go to. Psalms 18:2 says:

"The Lord is my rock and my fortress and my
deliverer, my God, my rock, in whom I take refuge, my shield, and the
horn of my salvation, my stronghold."

You are right that events and people cannot be completely relied on, but He can be. Even when you cannot see His plan in something that happens, trust His character that He is working out the best sequence of events for His glory but also for you. Maybe the gift you need to give Him today is the relinquishment of your desire for control over some person or situation in your life. Just as He promised Jacob to always be with him, He has promised over and over to be with you. You already have the blessing. Now is the time to relinquish control and give Him the acknowledgment and trust He deserves.

I talked to a Christian woman with a vibrant and exciting faith last night. She had prayed aloud a prayer of thanks to the Lord that was so profoundly from the depths of her soul and so overflowing with gratitude that my heart had been moved, and I mentioned it to her after our Wednesday prayer meeting at church. She said that when she was young, her husband had died leaving her with four small children. She was devastated and completely unprepared to raise the children alone, provide for herself, and just go on with such immense grief. With God's help, she has raised to adulthood some of the most Godly and accomplished young people I know. She said, "I wish I could go back thirty years and tell my younger self that God really is faithful and that He really will walk with her and see her through and show her how it all turns out."

You can tell yourself now that with God by your side, it (whatever the "it" is in your life) all turns out well because He will be with you. That is a promise.

DEVOTIONAL 4: LORD, I AM WILLING, PART 1

Our children are brilliant rebels. They know exactly how to go about pushing back against the rules in a way that tempts us to cave in or lose our tempers or in some way fail to be models of Christlike behavior. They are also masters of strategy, developing the ability at a disturbingly early age to intuit the moment when we are most vulnerable for them to start their shenanigans.

Case in point: When my son Houston was three, he was always the life of the party (still is.) He wanted to be the first to arrive and the last to leave. That last part was often the crux of an ongoing tug-of-war-between us. He never wanted to leave play group, birthday parties, or visits with friends. He is a straightforward kind of guy, so he usually was pretty direct and vocal about not wanting to go and would try to wrangle out of my arms if I tried to overrule him and just take him out. He found out from many trials that these tactics did not work. One day we met my mother, my sister, and Houston's adored cousins at the mall. A good time was had by all, but finally, I said to my three-year old son, "Let's go." With steely determination in his eyes, he staunchly said, "NO!" But this day, he tried a new technique. When I firmly took his hand and said we were leaving, he let his entire body go limp. He was VERY big for his age and built like a football player. He knew there were limits of what I could lift with my weak back. Even more shrewdly, he knew that I do not like to attract attention to myself in public and would be appalled at the idea of a real scene between us in the center of the mall. He was right about that, but he underestimated my motivation. I knew that if I let this young rebel outfox me with this tactic, all hope was lost when I would make future tries to leave the mall or other places. The physical battle was fierce, but I finally dragged his limp and protesting body into the stairwell of the mall and away from the people who had stopped to stare at this mom wrangle *and almost be defeated by* a toddler! I was too exhausted for several minutes to get all the way to the car!

We are exactly like that. Brilliant rebels. Looking for our outs and justifications so we can get our way.

And most of us sin against God in the same way. We have read our Bibles enough not to fight with Him head on. Instead, we let our minds and hearts go slack. We may not appear to be working directly against him, but our apathy, our not making ourselves wholly available to Him, and our lack of initiative to pursue Him with all of our hearts reminds me of the limp body of my son who was forcing me to drag him where I wanted him to go.

What about you? Are you in prayer about the exciting things God might be doing in your vicinity and are you rushing forward to make sure you let Him use you to advance His plans? Is every muscle and limb at his service, aligned with Him so He can move you easily to the place He wants you to go? Is your mind stayed on the Word and prepared in prayer so when He says, "Let's go," you are ready and rushing out the door to serve as He sees fit, not just in a role convenient for you? Are you ready to go, even though there is someplace else you want to be?

Most of us falter at times in our intentionality to live foremostly for Him and not for ourselves or our families. We allow our passion for His purposes or our fervency in prayer to weaken.

Contrast that with Jesus. God got ready for Jesus to leave the earth. Jesus was headed toward pain, suffering, death, humiliation, and temporary separation from His beloved Father after thousands of years of togetherness. Yet the Father said, "Let's go." What was Jesus' response?

"Father, if you are willing, remove this cup from me. Nevertheless, not my will, but yours, be done." Luke 22:42

Jesus negates His own will when he says "not my will." He relinquishes wholly any right to his own will with that "NOT." He asks the Lord to remove the cup only if the Father is "willing."

Pray that the Lord will give you the heart impulse to relinquish your will and to go where He is willing for you to go. Tell the Lord, "I am willing."

And in case you don't know me, I love my wonderful son beyond reason, the same one who was a rebellious three-year old. And God loves you, His child, even more than that-- even when you are balky, even when you sin, even when you disappoint yourself and others.

Nothing could change the love I have for my son and nothing will stop God from loving you.

DEVOTIONAL 5: "LET IT BE TO ME ACCORDING TO YOUR WORD."

From Luke 1: 26-56

One of the most beautiful responses to the Lord is that of Mary the mother of Jesus when she is told she will become pregnant, even though she is a virgin. This is a shocking circumstance in her day. Women had been stoned for less. Luke gives us the full picture of Mary's astonishing answer to God's decision to turn her life upside down.

Up to this point, it seems that Mary is considered the typical Jewish young lady, a good girl but with no supernatural attributes. She is going about her routine life when the angel Gabriel breaks into her day to say:

"Greetings, you who are highly favored! The Lord is with you." **29** *Mary was greatly troubled at his words and wondered what kind of greeting this might be.* **30** *But the angel said to her, 'Do not be afraid, Mary; you have found favor with God.* **31** *You will conceive and give birth to a son, and you are to call him Jesus.* **32** *He will be great and will be called the Son of the Most High. The Lord God will give him the throne of his father David,* **33** *and he will reign over Jacob's descendants forever; his kingdom will never end.'* **34** *'How will this be,' Mary asked the angel, 'since I am a virgin?'"*

35 *"And the angel answered her, 'The Holy Spirit will come upon you, and the power of the Most High will overshadow you; therefore the child to be born will be called holy—the Son of God.* **36** *And behold, your relative Elizabeth in her old age has also conceived a son, and this is the sixth month with her who was called barren.* **37** *For nothing will be impossible with God.'*

In about a minute, Mary goes from being troubled and afraid to this response:

38 *And Mary said, 'Behold, I am the servant of the Lord;* **let it be to me according to your word...'"** *Luke 1:28b-38*

This yielding in submission takes my breath away. This immediate acceptance is shocking. Surely this must be one of the reasons God chose Mary. She knows that people will talk about her, and that she will be disgraced. And I cannot even imagine what her thoughts were about the difficult conversation she was about to have with her fiancé who had been patiently waiting to marry her. But her words are completely submissive: *"let it be to me according to your word..."*

This is not how she had planned her life to be. A wedding to Joseph was on her calendar, not an unexpected pregnancy. Her agenda, vision for her future, place in the community, all of that went up in smoke when she unhesitatingly embraced what God wanted from her.

As I was writing this today, my son called and spontaneously asked me to lunch. His job rarely allows much of a lunch hour for him, but today is MLK Day and few people were in the office. I was telling him excitedly about the blog and how I was enjoying this assignment. He said (to me *out of nowhere*), "If writing the blog led to more speaking at churches, would you do that?" It was an innocent question, but God was using it to confront something inside me. I love the speaking I have done, but the way he phrased it indicated more travel. I stumbled and stammered over my answer and then just paused so I could give an honest response. Finally, I said, "I don't want to make an idol of my comfort and ease, and I do want to serve God in whatever way He decides. If that is what He decides, then I would be willing."

My son knows I am a real homebody. The fact that his chatty Mom was temporarily at a loss for words at his question told him something in me was resisting saying "yes," but did not want to give him a glib answer. By the time my lips struggled to come up with the words, "I would be willing," I meant it because I knew there was a reason I had been writing about Mary's willingness prior to our lunch. God was speaking to me through Luke 1 and then through my son.

What are some barriers for you when God wants something from you? Your schedule, your image of how your life or family should look like, doubts about your usefulness, the things you value on earth, your own vision of how you will serve Him? Can you say to Him with complete conviction, *"Let it be to me according to your word?"*

14

Let's pray together this week that we will all submit as Mary did, no matter the cost. Let's pray about the areas where we know we are weak that might be barriers to our saying, *"**Let it be to me according to your word?**"*

DEVOTIONAL 6: LORD, I AM WILLING, PART II

Today is the final part of this series of glimpses into some people's lives who said to God, "I am willing."

How fitting that the final and best example of willingness to conform to the Father is His son, Jesus Christ. The impressive thing about Jesus is that despite His wonderful perfection, He unhesitatingly submitted to His Father. He was, and remains, our model for submission.

But for me personally, the loveliest part of Jesus' willingness is His willingness towards **_us_**. He was willing to help anyone: leper, sinner, persecutor, immoral women, me, anyone.

Everyone avoided lepers for social, religious, and health reasons, but not Jesus. When a leper approached Jesus, this was His response:

*"**3** Jesus reached out his hand and touched the man. 'I am willing,' he said. 'Be clean!' Immediately he was cleansed of his leprosy." Matthew 8:3 NIV*

Those words "I am willing" come to my mind often when I get in a stew about something or worry about my health or my family. I hear Him saying, "I am willing."

As we have seen, the Lord also wants us to be willing. Most of us struggle to desire His will over our own. We are willful. When Our Father created us, He knew this struggle would be a downside to giving us the ability to choose to do His will or go with our betraying hearts. Our view of any circumstance is unreliable, near-sighted, and biased. His view and His will leads only to our future best and is reliable, far-sighted, and perfect.

God knew we would use our will imperfectly and wrongly at times. That is why He offered His Son, making provision to cover all of our sin and the damage we might try to cause to our relationship with Him and to ourselves. That is why Jesus, even when we are unloving toward Him, loves us more than anyone in our lives and willingly died for us—for you, specifically. If you want to know more about this, please email me at ChristianityAdventures@gmail.com or ask your questions to the wonderful women who comment at the end of my blog, AdventuresinChristianity.net.

Take a moment to really think about the following verses that will encourage you to say to the Lord, "I am willing." Might one of these apply to your children, a relationship, your finances, your Bible study, your teaching, your service to the Lord, a habit, the use of your time, or some other part of your life? Which verse speaks to you or do you have one of your own you want to post?

_____

_____

If you are willing and obedient, you will eat the good things of the land; Isaiah 1:19

Be shepherds of God's flock that is under your care, watching over them—not because you must, but because you are willing, as God wants you to be; not pursuing dishonest gain, but eager to serve. 1 Peter 5:2

Watch and pray so that you will not fall into temptation. The spirit is willing, but the flesh is weak.   Mark 14:38

For if the willingness is there, the gift is acceptable according to what one has, not according to what one does not have.   Corinthians 8:12

Prayer for today

Restore to me the joy of your salvation and grant me a willing spirit, to sustain me.   Psalm 51:12

DEVOTIONAL 7: THE LOVE OF YOUR LIFE

An Atlanta pastor began a wedding recently by telling the bride and groom, "This is not the most important relationship in your life."

This week, you may be thinking about love because of Valentine's Day. You may have it on your mind because you have a husband or fiancée who loves you with romantic love and are hoping that there are chocolates or flowers or a beautiful card in your future. Or you may be surrounded by friends as I am this year who celebrate friendships with a meal together and sometimes childlike or funny Valentine's cards. Or you may have family members who express their love to you.

As fun as all of this is, no form of love can touch the depth, the extravagance, the costly value, and the comfort of the love the Lord has for you. I have had each of the types of love mentioned above at one time or another in my life. All have failed me at times. God's love is the only love that never flags, weakens, takes a vacation, or fails to hold me up. I live embraced in His love, and whether you know it or not, so do you. It is the most important relationship in your life.

To take a step out of the ordinary for just a moment and to savor the extraordinary love of God, let's go to the Source, Himself. What does He say about who He is and about His love for us?

Love by the numbers

- Love is mentioned in the Bible almost 700 times using the word, but it is mentioned thousands of times by the stories it tells and by God's actions on our behalf.
- And God does not love us marginally. He tells us at least a dozen times that He is "abounding in love" for us.
- He is not going away. He tells us over 200 times that His love is steadfast; over 50 times that His love will endure forever. No human love can promise that.

How good is God's love?

How good is God's love? A psalmist who knew God well said, "It is better than life." In another place, the psalmist says God's love "reaches to the heavens" and His "faithfulness reaches to the skies." It is big love. It is so vast, humans cannot duplicate it or fully understand it.

I love the way Zephaniah describes God and His exultant love for us in 3:17:

"...He will rejoice over you with gladness; he will quiet you by his love; he will exult over you with loud singing."

Now that last part, "loud singing," needs some explanation. I am told that English has no word that conveys what God does here as He overflows with the joy of His love for us. Some translations say He is dancing and singing over us. Some say it is a leap of joy combined with singing. While we are going about the mundane events of our lives, God's heart is being moved with such love for us that He has these bursts of rejoicing over us—and not because we do anything to deserve it. His love for us is unconditional. He loved the thief on the cross who died beside Jesus who never taught a Bible study, never prayed, never worked for the Lord, never attended church, and was a criminal, as much as He loved Billy Graham. Amazing that His love comes from Him and not from us. Because it is a love that emanates from Him, it is perfect and can never end.

Please do not deprive your days and your thoughts and your soul of this love just because the world has put trouble in your path. God told us the world would do that (John 16:33.) But He also told us that He had overcome the world. Partake in that! In addition to what the world throws at us, He may even lovingly discipline us as we discipline the children we want everything for. Proverbs 3:12 says that "the Lord disciplines those He loves, as a father the son he delights in." But that is as much an act of love as the singing and the blessing.

What does God want from us?

God wants everything and needs nothing. He want us to love Him with every fiber of our hearts, souls, minds, and bodies. But He will not lack anything He needs if we don't. His kind of loving is to bless us, not Him. Jesus once answered the question above as He was being grilled by a Pharisee. He told the man what we all are to do:

"…You shall love the Lord your God with all your heart and with all your soul and with all your mind. This is the great and first commandment." Matthew 22:37-38

God teaches us a lot about His rich love for us and the way He wants us to love Him passionately in the book, Song of Solomon. He tells you to "set me as a seal upon your heart, as a seal upon your arm, for love is strong as death, jealousy is fierce as the grave. Its flashes are flashes of fire, the very flame of the Lord."(8:6) He tells you to *"let him lead (you) to the banquet hall, and let his banner over (you) be love. (2:4)*

Will you let Him put His banner over you and cover you with His love? Every protection, every joy, every blessing, every way out can be found under that banner. Please let Him lead you today. You just have to say, "Yes."

Do you know someone who needs true love? Please share this message of love today with anyone who might be blessed by receiving this love letter.

DEVOTIONAL 8: EIGHT THINGS WOMEN TAKE FROM GOOD TO BAD

With our unique gifting from the Lord, women definitely make anyplace they inhabit a better place. Our families, our houses, our churches, our neighborhoods, and our workplaces would not be nearly as delightful if all the women were to leave well enough alone.

We like to make things better. We like to embellish and add layers of comfort. We want to make things more appealing to the eye, the ear, and the tastebuds. It is part of who we are.

And just ask our children or spouses—we like to improve things, situations, and, most of all, people. And if we don't see progress happening fast enough, we will try to move things along. Read the last three paragraphs aloud to your siblings, children, spouses, or other family and see if they agree.

Overall, our self-appointed commission to make the world a better place is a good thing; however, satan loves to take any good thing and take it to a place it was never meant to go and change it to a bad thing. That is what he does with our impulse to improve everyone and everything around us. Below are eight things I see Christians taking from good to bad. Each of these has a good purpose in God's Kingdom, but our fallen nature has found ways to pervert the good purpose and apply it wrongly. Or are you perhaps just taking a good thing a tad too far? I know the ones below with my name on them. Do you?

1.   Yearning

God put yearning in us. Our primary yearning, whether we realize it or not, is for Him. Blaise Pascal called this the God-shaped void that is in us that nothing else will fill or satisfy. Often we see women trying to fill up the void of their loneliness and emptiness with food, alcohol, social activities, shopping, desire for attention, sex, social media, phone conversations, or any number of insufficient substitutes. Even an overabundance of church or community activities is the wrong way to satisfy the void and is a distraction from His voice and the walk He wants with us. Our desperation to fill the void ironically keeps us so frantically busy we do not allow Him into our souls and our lives the way He wants to abide there. The Lord wants time with us and wants our faces turned toward His in prayer. We have to be sure we allow Him to take the lead in what we will do for Him and how we will spend our time with Him. He does not need a laundry list of service projects; He needs us in His presence. He wants Mary time not Martha time.

2.   Romantic or physical love

One aspect of yearning is for romantic or physical love. Some women wreck a perfectly beautiful life God has given them in pursuit of the kind of love in Hallmark movies or in romantic novels. The intensity and self-gratification of that kind of love is pretty heady stuff. Pursuing it takes time, energy, and focus.

Again, yearning is a good thing, put there by God for His purposes. Genesis 3:16 says, *"To the woman he said, "I will surely multiply your pain in childbearing; in pain you shall bring forth children. Your desire shall be for your husband, and he shall rule over you."*

But if our time, energy, and focus are more on our desire for romance or sex than on our desire to glorify God, we have gotten out of balance. We need to be prayerfully restored in our hearts to a place where loving Him and being in His presence is the satisfying condition of our lives. Whatever God gifts us with beyond that is an added blessing.

Some of the most content and joyous people I know are women who never married or who have been widowed or divorced for decades. Most of these wanted to marry at one time, but their prayer for their lives was for God's will, first and foremost. God has given my first mentor and Christian friend an incredible ministry to those in Atlanta with AIDS (since 1986) and to their families. As she has shared Christ with them, she experiences so much love and joy. Though unmarried and with no biological children, she now has many "sons and daughters" who treat her like a mom and who, now that she is older, serve her as she serves them.

I also have friends who have made an idol of romantic love. They are some of the most unhappy people I know. Our society has depicted the Prince Charmings who are to come into our lives so unrealistically, that one can understand how women are disappointed when life does not imitate the romance in movies and television. The disappointment of many married women is also intensified this way and through books and self-help literature that intensify the message that we deserve more from men in the romance and support areas. But more on that in a later blog.

3.   Service

Although I covered service as a substitute for His presence above, I cannot state strongly enough that acts of service are no substitute for loving Him, loving others as Jesus loves you, and being obedient to only the things He has called you to do.

I Samuel 15:22 says, *"And Samuel said, 'Has the LORD as great delight in burnt offerings and sacrifices, as in obeying the voice of the LORD? Behold, to obey is better than sacrifice, and to listen than the fat of rams.' "*

Whatever you do in service for the Lord, be sure you do it out of love for Him and His children. Step back if you are only doing a service out of guilt or the inability to say "no." Also, if your busy-ness in service is causing you to neglect your family and bringing your children up in the nurture and admonition of the Lord, you need to take a long look at what you are really supposed to be doing. Please don't misunderstand, I do believe you can serve your church while your children are young, but be vigilant about too much of a good thing.

4.   A Season of Service – Knowing when a season is over

I have shared before the wonderful Prayer Team God allowed me to serve on for many years. It was delightful, service and the fellowship I experienced with that team of women still warms me when I think of it. But as the prayer needs of our church grew, handling prayer requests for hundreds of women created an administrative element to the role I played. Administration is NOT one of my gifts. I labored to keep up. Sometimes we would have events with 600 women attending. It was important to me that we not lose any prayer requests and that we pray in agreement over every one. That meant making copies for the partners who prayed for each request. By looking at the handwritten requests, we could often learn something about the woman. Sometimes we could identify the handwriting of a young girl or of a very elderly person. It was so dear. Sometimes the long list of requests on one card could show you the pressures from so many areas a woman was going through. The copies allowed each prayer partner to see a bit of the woman's identity in her handwritten request, so those copies served a purpose. I have a neurological problem that makes standing in one place very painful, but I would stand at that copier as long as it took to get the requests prepared for our prayer time.

Separate from the Prayer Team, women from my church would sometime ask if I would pray for them about a specific prayer request. I began to notice that the administrative part of preparing for prayer was making it more and more difficult to find the time to actually spend a sufficient amount of time in the Lord's presence, unhurried, for these women. Something was very wrong with that.

Ironically, I needed to resign from my administrative role on Prayer Team to have more time to pray. The season was over for me to pray in agreement on that wonderful team that serves the women and serves the Lord so beautifully even today. He was calling me to spend more time in interceding in prayer.

Many women have a problem with false guilt. Sometimes God moves us from one area of service to another. He may even give us a rest in between. Some of us have a difficult time leaving a service we have done for Him. When this happens, ask God what He is calling you to do. And sometimes, you can see that God has someone else prepared who has been called to take on the role you are leaving. Seeing others take your former responsibility with a fresh calling from God is so encouraging. God does not always show you why He has brought change into your life, but when He does, you get a glimpse of His plan.

5.   Church social versus forsaking the gathering together

Women have to find the right balance between spending time in fellowship with other women versus focusing on fellowship with the

Lord. Our Father created us for fellowship both with each other and with Him. Some of us tend to spend an extreme amount of time on just one of those and begin to neglect the other. Do you have a tendency to fellowship with fellow Christians but neglect spending regular quality time alone in the presence of your Father? Or are you on the other end of the spectrum like me, spending lots of time in private praise and prayer but being in danger of forsaking fellowship with other Christians on a consistent basis? Hebrews 10:24-25 says *24 And let us consider how to stir up one another to love and good works, 25 not neglecting to meet together, as is the habit of some, but encouraging one another, and all the more as you see the Day drawing near.*

Church should never be reduced to a social function, and we should not be running from activity to activity, but church should be a mainstay in our week. Fellowship with the saints will strengthen us in all kinds of ways. Which end of the spectrum do you tend to swing toward or do you have a good balance?

6.   Love of children and other family members

Clearly, God loves families. He invented them! Family love is one of His most beautiful ideas, but some women can get confused and think that their love and relationship with their family is their god. We are accountable to God for loving Him and bringing Him glory before we are accountable for spending all of our energy on our family. All of our time and resources belong to Him first. Our first love should be for the Lord. Taking family love to the extreme that we have limited energy or time left for prayer and quiet time with the Lord is not a balanced approach and does not benefit anyone in the long run. This teaching does not give us an excuse to neglect our families, but if we start with giving Him His due, He will expand our time and ensure everything that is important will get done. In the pursuit of either of these ends of the spectrum, we should not be legalistic. He will give us Grace till we figure it out. Just pray and ask Him to help you give Him and your family what He wants you to give. He knows this is a hard one and will help you.

7.   Meekness

There is a great word in the King James Version of the Bible—
"froward." Froward is more than being forward. It has an element of
wickedness. We are not to be too forward or froward. We are to be
strong and bold because our confidence is in the Lord, but that does
not mean we should be pushy. When you know for sure the outcome
of every little and big thing is in God's capable hands, you can rest
and not strive.

Jesus calls us to be meek. He gives us this strong incentive for
meekness:

"Blessed are the meek: for they shall inherit the earth." Matthew 5:5

And in Matthew 11:29, He tells us that He Himself is meek:

*"Take my yoke upon you, and learn of me; for I am meek and lowly in
heart: and ye shall find rest unto your souls."*

But meekness does not mean we do not take initiative to serve the
Lord. Meekness is not a license to be self-conscious, one of the many
"self-centered" sins. Self-consciousness, taken a step too far, is
another way to draw attention to yourself and even make your own
fears and emotions an idol you serve. Meekness does not mean we
are hyper-aware of how we are feeling when we are talking to others.
When you talk to others, focus on their comfort level and not your
own. *You can do all things through Christ who strengthens you*, so
you can talk to strangers or enter a room full of people. *Philippians
4:13*

Meekness is defined as power under control. As Christians, we should
not feel powerless. The very power that resurrected Jesus Christ is
available to us to help us through our situations in life. We should walk
in meekness, but always be aware that we have an inner strength that
is not from us but from Jesus Christ.

Walking in this confidence and power should not cross the line to
forwardness or forwardness. As with the other items on this list, we
have to find the balance between self-consciousness and
forwardness. The perfect balance is meekness.

"I therefore, the prisoner of the Lord, beseech you that ye walk worthy of the vocation wherewith ye are called,

2 With all lowliness and meekness, with longsuffering, forbearing one another in love;"

Ephesians 4:3

8.   Provision

A healthy attitude toward provision and possessions is needed by Christians. We have the most wonderful assurance that all of our needs will be met.

"And my God will supply every need of yours according to his riches in glory in Christ Jesus."

Philippians 4:19

Because of this and many other promises throughout the Scriptures, we do not need to:

·   Stress over bills or our financial future

·   Hoard or stack closets to protect ourselves out of fear

·   Eat too much at meals because of a fear of being deprived later

·   Worry if our savings is not as much as our neighbor's

·   Negotiate so hard we damage our witness

·   Deprive others of money through leaving unjust gratuities or pressing too hard for extra discounts

We should be modeling our confidence in a God who owns the cattle on a thousand hills, not looking desperate and fearful.

On the other hand, the Bible warns us about waste. It tells us that God is a God of order and that we are to be good stewards of what He has given us. We are told that a workman should be worthy of His hire. The lazy Christians in an office reflect badly on our Savior. Again, a Christian must find the balance between resting in the Lord about money and provision and the other end of the spectrum where people are often undisciplined about money and possessions.

I think back to a time when I was a child. In general, homes were smaller and there was a sweet intimacy about them. Back then, if you looked in most people's closets, you would not see them packed with clothes. People had fewer changes of clothes, making life much easier. Less was more.

Trust God to fulfill your needs and then pray that you will be content with the circumstances He gives you. Some of the most dissatisfied people I know have lavish wealth. Only God can satisfy. Turn the provision in your life over to Him today. He is trustworthy.

DEVOTIONAL 9: JUDGMENTALISM

I am easily shocked. That is who I am. I was brought up by a military father who loved me but was very strict. I thank God for **both** of those things. He was a stickler for etiquette and proper behavior in general. Even in first grade, I knew to answer the phone by saying all the caller needed to know: "Fitts residence. Casey speaking." He had the most sacrificial love for his family that I have ever encountered, and part of that love was to protect us by teaching us what life had taught him. He instilled in us an absolute fear of overstepping our bounds, being intrusive, venturing where we are not invited, and any number of elements in his code. My mother was charming and many people dropped in on us uninvited, which we knew was a big breach of etiquette in my Dad's book. And in some cases, these people truly were being rude as in the case of the neighbor who always happened to drop in right at dinnertime (my Dad was also a gourmet cook and our meals were exotic and sumptuous.)

All that to say, there are many reasons that as I walk down the street or shop in the stores or interact with acquaintances, I frequently experience these little sparks of shock at someone's bad language or rudeness or presumptuousness or insensitive remark or some small thing. I know that the real root of this is not my father but my judgmental spirit. My Dad just gave me the opportunity to use him as an excuse to be that way. It is a pride problem. It is a sin problem.

Because of our sin speckled hearts, we cannot anticipate when these thoughts come unbidden to the surface. They pop into our minds when we are not expecting them and are just there before we can mount a defense.

When that happens, I have learned a few things I can do to get out of judgment mode as fast as I can:

1. First, cast as hard and as fast as you can.

"6 Humble yourselves, therefore, under the mighty hand of God so that at the proper time he may exalt you, 7 casting all your anxieties on him, because he cares for you. 8 Be sober-minded; be watchful.

Your adversary the devil prowls around like a roaring lion, seeking someone to devour." 1 Peter 5:6-8

2. Look at the offending person as a child of God. If you have a child of your own, you know they are not perfect, no matter how wonderful they are. Still, we don't like for another person to criticize, judge, look down on, or shut out our child. Neither does God. He created the person in front of you, and He loves him or her very much. I might discipline my child for something he does, but I don't think it is appropriate for another mom to discipline my child the way I do. God feels the same way.

My sister who died at 58 of cancer was the most intelligent and gifted person I have ever known. Before the age of 12, she could play 7 musical instruments and was a virtuoso on the French horn. When she would pick up a new instrument, she would become that teacher's star pupil in a short period of time. My sister Bobbi and I were in awe of her gifts, as was anyone who met her.

But Jan became an alcoholic at 14, did drugs, and burned bridges with many people. She was my parents' favorite child, their baby, and their pride and joy, but at some point so much happened they had to take a break from having her in their home. They had depleted their savings sending her to every expensive treatment program in the south well into her forties, but her condition just got worse. The alcohol took its toll on her brain, and the mental illness that resulted took its toll on all of our lives, but hers most of all. Simultaneously, my parents got older and could not handle the things that were happening with her.

One wonderful event occurred in those years—she had a beautiful, brilliant son. That baby was the most prayed over baby that has ever been born, and despite her drinking entire bottles of wine during most of her pregnancy, he had not a trace of fetal alcohol syndrome. Tell me prayer doesn't work! He was healthy, athletic, and extremely intelligent. Through too many horrific events to describe, Jan lost him to DFACs. My other sister Bobbi and her husband Wayne have raised Zach as their son and their beautiful devotion to him shows in the confident, Godly man he is today.

Bobbi says that she got Zach and I got Jan, because at about this time, an incident happened when Jan was visiting my parents that led to their not being able to have her in their home for an extended period. My parents, however, looked to me to be family to Jan since they were not strong enough at that time to be there for her.

I will say that she was witty and interesting and lots of fun to be with when she was sober, so I enjoyed much of the time with her. She was my movie buddy. One of the many jobs she held was as a restaurant reviewer (Jan could always land a job because she was a gifted conversationalist, sales professional, and writer.) Still, there were times my friend Frances and I would have to go rescue her from horrible situations she had gotten herself into. We once had to go into what looked like a shrine to satan because she was passed out there, and her counselor called and thought she might stop breathing from an alcohol overdose. It had happened twice before, and one of the times led to a tracheotomy to save her life. I only share this with you to tell you that Jan was one of God's children whose sins were just very public and showed more than my sins of judgmentalism and pride that I am confessing here.

Of course, I invited Jan to church and Christian events and to do things with my Christ-like friends. On rare occasions she went. Of course, I talked to her about my faith. I had been a wild child early on and could talk with her as one who had sinned greatly and was only different through God's grace. She had been very much against Christianity because she equated it with judgment. By God's grace, she could see dramatic change in me, and I will always be grateful that she knew my relationship with the Lord was real because nothing else could explain the transformation she watched happen. We talked openly about the things of the Lord, and I believe she was saved when she died.

Still, her lifestyle was unhealthy and her choices continued to leave her in terrible circumstances. Being the firstborn, my impulse was to change her. I was always buying her new clothes to go on job interviews and giving her pep talks and trying to reason her out of her self-destructive behavior. One day I was praying about it, and God rebuked me for all my busy-ness in meddling in Jan's life. I clearly understood Him to speak into my heart and say (not audibly), "She is not your child. She is my child. She is not yours to change. If there is to be a change, the Holy Spirit will do that. Your only job is to love her."

What a relief! Jan was eight years younger. Because of my mother's hospitalizations and illnesses, I had been her babysitter for fifty years! God relieved me of that and allowed me to just be her sister for those last years of her life. Sure, I still occasionally gave her money to get her car fixed or to help out from time to time, but not with the expectation attached that she would change—just a gift because I loved her.

But God used Jan in my life to teach me a new way to look at people and catch myself mid-judgment to say to myself, "She is not my child. She is God's child, and He loves her very much. He will deal with her and discipline her. It is not up to me to think about what should happen and what ought to happen. A parent knows his or her child better than anyone. Certainly, God knows what needs to happen here." And I can turn people over to God more quickly now because of my beloved sister Jan.

3. Here is a verse that will help you drop that critical spirit fast as you can:

"14 For if you forgive others their trespasses, your heavenly Father will also forgive you, 15 but if you do not forgive others their trespasses, neither will your Father forgive your trespasses." Matthew 6:14-15

And the Lord's Prayer continues this principle for hearts that are truly conformed to His:

"4 Forgive us our sins, for we also forgive everyone who sins against us." Luke 11:4 NIV

4. When your mind or heart jumps to judgment, this is the ultimate moment to ask yourself, "What would Jesus do if He were here looking at this person right now?" You only need to think of the Samaritan woman and other outcasts Jesus interacted with to know His response to people might be far more loving than yours or mine.

DEVOTIONAL 10: WHY NOT?

I was sitting in church a few weeks ago, minding my own business when I was gobsmacked! [1] Has that ever happened to you? Suddenly a verse our pastor was drawing our attention to leapt off the page and hit me in the face. I knew God was speaking forcefully to me and not to the general congregation. And I knew He meant business. I guess you could say I was God-smacked.

Our pastor, Michael Youssef, was teaching on I Corinthians 6:7:

7 *The very fact that you have lawsuits among you means you have been completely defeated already. Why not rather be wronged? Why not rather be cheated? NIV*

The part the Lord hit me between the eyes with was the middle part: **Why not rather be wronged?**

Wha-a-a-t? Why not be wronged? Well, for a million reasons. Why would I want to be wronged? That goes against everything I have learned in this world. I don't want to be wronged. (I hope you read that last sentence in the plaintive, defiant, shocked, and whiney voice my sinful heart was saying it in!) I don't want someone to detract from my reputation or tell untruths about me. I should be able to defend myself, right? That is only just and right—in the world's system.

My pastor made me see I had a clear choice in this matter: Would I rather defend myself or grow in my intimacy with the Lord? What would I let go of for greater intimacy with Him? Would I rather be proven right or be right with Him? The choice was so clear that I felt refreshed that Dr. Youssef had made it so easy to know what I had to do. And then the question made more sense. *Yes, why not?* What do I have to gain in this world that compares to the peace and joy that the Lord can give me? *Why not?* What can help my future more: my self-defense or letting it go and placing it in the flawlessly capable hands of my Father? *Why not?*

I feel this *"Why not?"* response will be part of my life from this point on. It is such a God-response. It is counterintuitive and goes against all conventional wisdom. It is so above that. It is the type of truth that sets captives free and brings the peace that passes understanding.

When a situation came up almost immediately (you know how our enemy likes to do that on the heels of a good sermon), I almost laughed out loud as I thought, "Why not rather be wronged here?" It is a joyous discovery.

You may think this is a ridiculously simple realization, but the "aha" moments I have about the Word are often like that. One minute it is a verse I have seen a hundred times, and the next minute I am seeing it as if for the first time, and it is changing my life in a whole new way. The Word is dynamic and mysterious and Divine that way.

And it does not mean that allowing ourselves to be wronged will be easy. The ESV version stresses that we will suffer for it:

7 *To have lawsuits at all with one another is already a defeat for you. Why not rather suffer wrong? Why not rather be defrauded?*

I will tell you that when God woke me up to the idea of experiencing a wrong and responding by saying, "Why not rather be wronged?, I felt this sense of relief. I felt as if I had set down a bag of rocks so heavy it was exhausting me to carry them. I was able to pray for those *who despitefully use me*[2] with such love and tenderness that I myself was refreshed in prayer. When I released that burden and in my heart joined Christ in saying, "Why not rather be wronged?", I felt that God and I walked out of that sanctuary together and I was walking with Him, matching Him stride for stride.

What about you? Have you ever been God-smacked by a verse? I would love to hear about it.

1. Gobsmacked. *Adjective.* British *slang:* astounded; astonished; from **Collins English Dictionary - Complete & Unabridged 2012 Digital Edition,** © William Collins Sons & Co. Ltd. 1979, 1986 © HarperCollins.

2. *Matthew 5:44. But I say unto you, Love your enemies, bless them that curse you, do good to them that hate you, and pray for them which despitefully use you, and persecute you;*

NOTE: *Asking a favor:* **I am trying to get the blog out to states outside of Georgia. Do you have friends who might want to try the blog? Do you have a mailing list you send things to? If your heart is so led, please send the link to the blog:**
https://www.adventuresinchristianity.net

DEVOTIONAL 11: FELLOW STRUGGLERS & VICTORS

I never want what I publish to seem to be saying that I have moved past my weaknesses and have grasped Grace so deeply that I don't struggle and fail. Believe me, I fail. For the next few weeks, we will look at the lives of some of our fellow strugglers from the Bible. We will get to know perhaps the most famous female sinner of all time today. Then for two weeks, we will look at the life of Reuben, brother of Joseph. We will see how God has chosen some of the most unlikely people to include in His holy Word, because they illustrate what He can do in a life through His Grace and love. He changes strugglers like us into victors.

I intentionally share my failures and what God is doing in my life because I feel that many Christian women feel that they are lagging behind in some kind of spiritual race. That is a lie from the enemy. We all struggle. I will battle my sin daily, submitting it to the Lord, until the day I join Jesus in Heaven and claim the victory that has already been won.

Just the other day, I was in a restaurant having the first morning just to myself in a couple of months. I had been speaking during the week, and every weekend held events that I wanted to support but that did not allow for the down time this introvert desperately needs. I had also been eating on the run or eating with clients and was looking forward to sitting alone, slowly having a meal while I read the previous Sunday's paper in total, delicious solitude. I chose a quiet place to steal away and have this hour of quiet and relaxation I had been looking forward to for weeks. About the time I began my meal, a table full of very masculine looking women with traditionally male haircuts and with piercings everywhere came and sat nearby. They appeared to be body builders and made it clear they were tough- tough talking, arms swinging women. I was comfortable with that because I know some amazing Christians who look just like this, but these women were not Christians. And they were loud—very loud. Each one seemed to want to outdo the other in the use of profanity and using the Lord's name in vain. The vulgarity was nonstop. Their main topic of conversation was ridiculing the Christians in their families, and each shared a different story to prove their belief that Christians were idiots, and mean-spirited idiots at that. They incorrectly referenced Bible stories they had been taught, including one who talked about her grandmother telling her about Noah and the burning bush.

Of course, enjoying a meal while our precious Lord's name was being profaned was impossible. This attack on Him was so overt and raucous, but I knew the Lord had seated me near them for a purpose. I knew He wanted these daughters of His to feel His love and to know Him, and that He wanted me to love them too. I decided that I would just sit there and pray while they were talking. But the Lord wanted more than that. He wanted me to approach them and extend kindness. How could I do this after what they had said? I felt they would just want to debate and that with the four of them the conversation would be counterproductive. I felt God gave me the insight that individually these women would listen to me, but they had formed a team against Christians, and that they would not back down in front of one another. How could I reach each one individually?

I remembered that I still had a box of books in my car from a speaking engagement. My book **Adventures in Christianity** gives an account of who God is and the amazing things He has done for me in my life. It is a book that shares my imperfections and struggles, but how God has loved me and brought me close to Him despite myself. It was a book I felt that each one of these scarred women could relate to. I went to the car and got a book for each one. I waited until they had finished their meal so as not to interrupt. On my way out the door, I went up to them and said, "Your stories of your mothers and grandmothers, and the Bible stories you mentioned really moved my heart. I am a local author, and I hope you don't mind if I give you one of my books. I mentor young women and would love to share this gift with you. Will you accept one?" I said this as I was already placing the books in their hands and they were reflexively accepting.

They were very quiet and a bit confused but each one seemed pleased and not hostile. I left the books with them and told them goodbye and that I hoped they continued to enjoy their day. Nothing I said was innovative or particularly strong, but I saw a softening in their faces as I talked to them. Honestly, I had expected to be cursed and yelled at. But the Holy Spirit did something to gentle them. And the work was not just in them, it was in me. You see, I did not want to go up to that table. I wanted to anonymously sit where I was and pray from a safe distance. Sometimes that is the answer, but sometimes He wants us to engage as He did with the woman at the well. That is the story He reminded me of when I first started eavesdropping on these women. He showed me His heart for them. But what was more moving to me was that He showed me His heart for me. He made me see that I was a sinner like these women and that He sent people to talk to me in my sin and to reach me, too. I am the woman at the well (This story from John 4:1-42 is copied for you at the end of this blog.) I thank God that strangers (now friends) like my friends Frances and Margaret were willing to see beyond who I was because they could see who I could be in Christ. They reached out to me even though I was a pistol! He flooded me that day with gratitude that people did not walk a wide circle around me but reached out to me.

I gave each woman a book with my name on it before they knew what hit them and let them know I was local. I am not that hard to find.

No one came to salvation that day (that I know of), but I do know that there have been unchurched people who have come to salvation after reading that book. I pray for these women from time to time that God will send more worthy laborers into their lives or that the book or a sermon they hear on the radio will draw them to Him. Instead of judging these women or holding on to my offense at their remarks, God has put a love in my heart for them.

Below are a few other verses to bolster you the next time the hair stands up on the back of your neck or your eyes widen in surprise at another person's remark or behavior. I will leave you with these verses that will help you not be easily offended:

Luke 6:31-42

31 Do to others as you would have them do to you. 32 "If you love those who love you, what credit is that to you? Even sinners love those who love them. 33 And if you do good to those who are good to you, what credit is that to you? Even sinners do that. 34 And if you lend to those from whom you expect repayment, what credit is that to you? Even sinners lend to sinners, expecting to be repaid in full. **35** But love your enemies, do good to them, and lend to them without expecting to get anything back. Then your reward will be great, and you will be children of the Most High, because he is kind to the ungrateful and wicked. **36** Be merciful, just as your Father is merciful. **37** "Do not judge, and you will not be judged. Do not condemn, and you will not be condemned. Forgive, and you will be forgiven. **38** Give, and it will be given to you. A good measure, pressed down, shaken together and running over, will be poured into your lap. For with the measure you use, it will be measured to you." **39** He also told them this parable: "Can the blind lead the blind? Will they not both fall into a pit? **40** The student is not above the teacher, but everyone who is fully trained will be like their teacher. **41** "Why do you look at the speck of sawdust in your brother's eye and pay no attention to the plank in your own eye? **42** How can you say to your brother, 'Brother, let me take the speck out of your eye,' when you yourself fail to see the plank in your own eye? You hypocrite, first take the plank out of your eye, and then you will see clearly to remove the speck from your brother's eye.

I Peter 3:15

but in your hearts honor Christ the Lord as holy, always being prepared to make a defense to anyone who asks you for a reason for the hope that is in you; yet do it with gentleness and respect,

James 4:11-12

11 Do not speak evil against one another, brothers. The one who speaks against a brother or judges his brother, speaks evil against the law and judges the law. But if you judge the law, you are not a doer of the law but a judge. **12** There is only one lawgiver and judge, he who is able to save and to destroy. But who are you to judge your neighbor?

Proverbs 11:12 NKJV

He who is devoid of wisdom despises his neighbor, But a man of understanding holds his peace.

JESUS AND THE WOMAN AT THE WELL

From John 4:4-42

4 Now when Jesus learned that the Pharisees had heard that Jesus was making and baptizing more disciples than John 2 (although Jesus himself did not baptize, but only his disciples), 3 he left Judea and departed again for Galilee. 4 And he had to pass through Samaria. 5 So he came to a town of Samaria called Sychar, near the field that Jacob had given to his son Joseph. 6 Jacob's well was there; so Jesus, wearied as he was from his journey, was sitting beside the well. It was about the sixth hour.[a]

7 A woman from Samaria came to draw water. Jesus said to her, "Give me a drink." 8 (For his disciples had gone away into the city to buy food.)9 The Samaritan woman said to him, "How is it that you, a Jew, ask for a drink from me, a woman of Samaria?" (For Jews have no dealings with Samaritans.) 10 Jesus answered her, "If you knew the gift of God, and who it is that is saying to you, 'Give me a drink,' you would have asked him, and he would have given you living water." 11 The woman said to him, "Sir, you have nothing to draw water with, and the well is deep. Where do you get that living water? 12 Are you greater than our father Jacob? He gave us the well and drank from it himself, as did his sons and his livestock." 13 Jesus said to her, "Everyone who drinks of this water will be thirsty again, 14 but whoever drinks of the water that I will give him will never be thirsty again.[b] The water that I will give him will become in him a spring of water welling up to eternal life." 15 The woman said to him, "Sir, give me this water, so that I will not be thirsty or have to come here to draw water."

16 Jesus said to her, "Go, call your husband, and come here." 17 The woman answered him, "I have no husband." Jesus said to her, "You are right in saying, 'I have no husband'; 18 for you have had five husbands, and the one you now have is not your husband. What you have said is true." 19 The woman said to him, "Sir, I perceive that you are a prophet.20 Our fathers worshiped on this mountain, but you say that in Jerusalem is the place where people ought to worship." 21 Jesus said to her, "Woman, believe me, the hour is coming when neither on this mountain nor in Jerusalem will you worship the Father. 22 You worship what you do not know; we worship what we know, for salvation is from the Jews.23 But the hour is coming, and is now here, when the true worshipers will worship the Father in spirit and truth, for the Father is seeking such people to worship him. 24 God is spirit, and those who worship him must worship in spirit and truth." 25 The woman said to him, "I know that Messiah is coming (he who is called Christ). When he comes, he will tell us all things." 26 Jesus said to her, "I who speak to you am he."

27 Just then his disciples came back. They marveled that he was talking with a woman, but no one said, "What do you seek?" or, "Why are you talking with her?" 28 So the woman left her water jar and went away into town and said to the people, 29 "Come, see a man who told me all that I ever did. Can this be the Christ?" 30 They went out of the town and were coming to him.

31 Meanwhile the disciples were urging him, saying, "Rabbi, eat." 32 But he said to them, "I have food to eat that you do not know about." 33 So the disciples said to one another, "Has anyone brought him something to eat?" 34 Jesus said to them, "My food is to do the will of him who sent me and to accomplish his work. 35 Do you not say, 'There are yet four months, then comes the harvest'? Look, I tell you, lift up your eyes, and see that the fields are white for harvest. 36 Already the one who reaps is receiving wages and gathering fruit for eternal life, so that sower and reaper may rejoice together. 37 For here the saying holds true, 'One sows and another reaps.' 38 I sent you to reap that for which you did not labor. Others have labored, and you have entered into their labor."

39 Many Samaritans from that town believed in him because of the woman's testimony, "He told me all that I ever did." 40 So when the Samaritans came to him, they asked him to stay with them, and he stayed there two days. 41 And many more believed because of his word. 42 They said to the woman, "It is no longer because of what you said that we believe, for we have heard for ourselves, and we know that this is indeed the Savior of the world."

DEVOTIONAL 12: REUBEN, A MAN OF GOOD INTENTIONS

I love Reuben. What a mess he is some days and what a valiant leader others. He is the stand-up guy who does the right thing most of the time, but from time to time, his flesh fails him and he sins. Big, revolting sins that he gets called out on.

Reuben is a mass of contradictions. I relate to him because I feel I am seeking the Lord pretty consistently most days, but then sin can take me unawares, and I find myself thinking thoughts or saying things that someone filled with the love of Christ just should not think or say. I wanted to study Reuben to understand where he failed in order to help me avoid some of his pitfalls. For selfish reasons, I wanted to understand how God looked at Reuben's sin and dealt with him. I found four defining moments that give me insight into why Reuben sinned, how he sinned, and God's take on it all.

1.   Reuben held the position of Jacob's firstborn of 12 sons, earning him a favored position in the family and the community, and a double portion of his inheritance when the time came. The first sin recorded for eternity in Reuben's life is fodder for the National Enquirer or Jerry Springer Show. He slept with his father's concubine, Bilhah. That slap in his father's face was intensely more disrespectful in 1900 BC than it is today. The sin was horrendous, but then all sin is. This one lost Reuben his birthright. He was no longer to be "enrolled" officially as Jacob's firstborn son. Instead, his brother Judah was given all the honor and privileges of this role.

2.   Reuben was right in there with his other brothers in hating his younger brother Joseph. Jacob made no secret of how brilliant and charming and wonderful Joseph was, buying him gifts like the famous coat of many colors, just because he was special. And Joseph, whether intentional or not, made the situation worse. With little discernment, he shared his dreams that portrayed how his brothers would someday bow down to him. And he was perceived as a tattletale. The brothers' resentment of Joseph grew intense as the years passed. One day, they saw their chance as they were tending sheep in a remote area and saw Joseph approaching. They determined to murder him. In this defining moment, Reuben stepped up and rescued him out of their hands. Reuben saw he could not

dissuade the angry mob of brothers from taking Joseph's life, so he tried a different strategy to buy some time until he could rescue Joseph. Being greatly outnumbered, Reuben had to be wily and said, " *'Shed no blood; throw him into this pit here in the wilderness, but do not lay a hand on him'—that he might rescue him out of their hand to restore him to his father." Genesis 37:22*

And they did, but without Reuben's knowledge, the brothers decided to sell Joseph to a band of merchants who just happened to come through at about that time.

To his credit, *"when Reuben returned to the pit and saw that Joseph was not in the pit, he tore his clothes." Genesis 37:29* Reuben's anguish is real when he thinks his father has forever lost his beloved son Joseph. Those sympathetic to Reuben feel he did all he could to oppose his brothers' plans to kill Joseph. Others feel he should have been more courageous and bolder to refuse to even put him in the danger of the pit. In any case, this episode ends with Reuben's being heartbroken for his enslaved (and assumed dead) brother, but seemingly more so for his bereaved father.

3.   Another defining moment when Reuben is the man he probably wanted to be in God's eyes occurred many years later. God orders his steps to face his brother Joseph again, whom he thought he would never see again and whom he believed dead. Because of God's sovereign will and the plans He had designed from the beginning of time for all of their lives, Joseph had worked his way up from slave to prisoner to the highest government position in the land of Egypt, second only to Pharaoh. In a twist of events only God could have orchestrated, his brothers have traveled to Egypt to meet with the highest official of the land to get grain because their people back home are starving. Though Joseph recognizes his older brothers, they do not recognize his face in this powerful and terrifying leader before them. He tells them to leave Simeon there and go home and bring back their younger brother Benjamin if they want more grain. He will execute Simeon if they do not return with Joseph's younger brother.

The older brothers return to their father and explain the situation, but Jacob cannot bear the thought of risking the loss of his son Benjamin and firmly refuses. Once again, Reuben steps up and makes an unthinkable offer to make things right. He says to his father, "Kill my two sons if I do not bring him back to you. Put him [Benjamin] in my hands, and I will bring him back to you."

What a passionate and sacrificial offer! Reuben is the kind of guy who will give all he has to rescue a brother. At first, Jacob refuses but eventually they must go to Egypt because the famine is continuing. The scene where the family is reunited and Joseph reveals his identity is one of the most emotional scenes in Scripture.

Reading this story for yourself, especially Genesis chapters 37, 42-25, will give you the many twists and turns of this emotional story, too long to cover here.

4.   Some scholars say that one of the flaws of Reuben's descendants was taking the easy way out sometimes. Critics base this primarily on a choice the Reubenites made to be one of the tribes to settle in Gilead before reaching the Promised Land. They looked at the land and thought it looked like a good place to raise livestock (their livelihood) and asked to be allowed to settle there. Were they right to take what looked like the easier way out to settle before taking the Promised Land? Were they opportunists who saw beautiful grazing land and felt that they found home? Or was this God's plan for them? You can find scholars who support each of these sides. What do you think?

Next week, we will take a closer look at Reuben's sin and the consequences. I will be interested in hearing your take on Reuben.

DEVOTIONAL 13: WHAT WERE THE CONSEQUENCES OF REUBEN'S SIN?

Last week, we looked at events that made up the four defining moments in Reuben's life. So what were the results? How did God deal with Reuben? What were the consequences? As we look at the four defining events below, we will also look at how God's Grace is clearly applied in every incident.

1.   Event one: Dishonoring his father.

Showing honor to your father or mother is a Bible basic. Showing honor to our fathers and mothers gives us practice in how to honor our Father in Heaven. Our Heavenly Father is perfect. Our earthly parents are not. Some of you may even have parents who were abusive, drug-addicted, criminal, or worse. You may not have been safe in your parent's home and had to leave. God understands that and is a wonderful parent to people whose earthly parents are unable or unwilling to parent well and love their children *(Read Psalm 27:10.)* But our words are not to be disrespectful about our parents, no matter their failings. For whatever reason, God chose those parents. Some of the most remarkable people I know grew to be that way out of terrible life beginnings. Their hardships and disappointments made them compassionate, wise, innovative, and strong. Never doubt that God has a plan for you and that He will use your pain in His ultimate, eternal plan for His kingdom and to bless you as part of it. And never believe false thoughts that God was not good to you or did not love you because you were given what seem to be unfair circumstances at the start of your life. God has *hope and a future* for you! *Jeremiah 29:11*

In Reuben's day, he was under the law, and the law was very strong about honoring your father. Reuben flagrantly disrespected his father Jacob when he slept with his concubine.

Of course, the consequence was losing the double portion of his father's estate, but more than that, he lost his position in Jacob's eyes and the eyes of his community. He was a fallen man, falling into sin and then falling in the standing and stature so important in that time. No matter how unfairly Jacob might have seemed to treat Reuben, remember that Reuben sinned against God when he broke the law. This was an even greater sin than dishonoring his father. We are not under the law today thanks to Jesus Christ, but the Bible is very clear that honoring our parents is close to the heart of God. Reuben knew this but allowed himself to give in to temptation.

GRACE POINT: But I see God being merciful to Reuben, even in this area of his life. Though Reuben loses the official position of firstborn, throughout the Bible, we see Reuben being the spokesperson for the family and being treated as a family leader. Certainly, he does this among his brothers when they want to kill Joseph. Again, when the brothers negotiate for Simeon's release in Egypt, Reuben seems to be a family leader alongside Judah. As Jacob is dying, he speaks at one point about Reuben's integrity (some versions call it his honor):

"Reuben, you are my firstborn, my might, and the firstfruits of my strength, preeminent in dignity and preeminent in power."

These words from Jacob make me think that though his was a life of highs and lows, Reuben overall led a life of integrity. Jacob does indicate that Reuben's sin with Bilhah will affect his ability to excel in the future, but he depends on his true firstborn in many ways.

Reuben's affair with Bilhah was an inexcusable offense, but apparently God allowed him to regain a place in Jacob's affections and a leadership position in the family. Only God's mercy could restore relationships like that to an undeserving man. Are you in a position of feeling undeserving of restoring a family relationship? Is there someone in your family who has broken relationship in such a hurtful way that they are undeserving? God's Grace can restore things that no human power can restore. Pray about the relationships in your family.

Throughout the rest of the Bible, the sons of Reuben are mentioned time after time. He made many mistakes, but God restored him as a leader and as a figure whose descendants figure prominently in Biblical history.

2.   Event two: Leaving Joseph in the pit.

Whether you think Reuben was a champion for trying to save Joseph or you think he was a cad for not standing up more strongly to his brothers, either way, Reuben was part of probably the worst sibling persecution I have ever heard about. I always think it is interesting to see what the Bible includes. The Bible is so economical that it often leaves out facts our curious natures would want to know, but in this case, a quote is included that reveals much to me about Reuben. When the brothers think they are in terrible trouble with Joseph in Egypt, Genesis 42:22 says: *"And Reuben answered them, 'Did I not tell you not to sin against the boy? But you did not listen. So now there comes a reckoning for his blood.' "*

GRACE POINT: The biggest point of Grace in this episode is that Joseph miraculously did not die in the pit. He did not die in prison when falsely accused by Potiphar's wife. Not only did he not die, he is raised through these very circumstances to the highest position in Egypt! It is the very act of persecution that takes him to the land he must go to in order to be elevated. Joseph understands how God uses our terrible circumstances and pain when he tells his brothers, *"As for you, you meant evil against me, but God meant it for good, to bring it about that many people should be kept alive, as they are today." Genesis 50:20*

Only God's Grace and complete forgiveness can take our mistakes and use them for our good and for the ultimate good of everyone involved.

3.   Event three: Facing Joseph in Egypt.

Joseph has driven a hard bargain with the brothers, and they are at an impasse. Joseph will not allow them to take back the grain to their starving families if they will not bring Benjamin to him. Brother Simeon is being held hostage to secure their return.

Benjamin is the younger brother of Joseph. Unlike the rest of the brothers, they share both the same mother and father. Benjamin now is Jacob's most cherished youngest son as Joseph once was. When the brothers first tell Jacob of the deal offered by Egypt and about Simeon's plight, Jacob cannot bear to let his Benjamin travel with the brothers because he remembers all too well what happened the last time he entrusted his youngest son to them. Initially, he says "no."

When Reuben offers to allow Jacob to kill his own two sons if he does not bring Benjamin back safe and sound, he shows a total commitment to protecting Simeon. Like us, he has learned from making regrettable mistakes and doubles his commitment to never make the same mistake again.

GRACE POINT: Reuben failed to protect Joseph from the brothers many years before. In God's very meaningful way of doing things, He allows Reuben to be the instrument to deliver Benjamin safely to Joseph and back home again to Jacob. God may not allow do-overs of our past sins, and we may experience consequences on earth, but He does show His grace by allowing us opportunities to do better in the future and to feel His pleasure when we do. In the end, God restores both of Jacob's younger sons to him, Joseph and Benjamin, and Simeon is safe as well.

4.   Event four: The consequences of Reuben's sin for his descendants.

As I mentioned, sometimes God will allow us to experience some consequences on earth for our sins. Although His Grace wipes away all guilt and shame, our actions can set in motion reactions from others. We sometimes have to live with those until we go home to meet Jesus. Some scholars say that appears to happen with Reuben's descendants who sometimes had a reputation for taking the easy way out. This reputation purportedly started when the sons of Reuben asked to settle east of the Jordan River, before arriving in the Promised Land.

Later on in Judges 4-5, the story of Deborah and Sisera does not paint a bold, brave picture of the sons of Reuben. As other tribes are praised for going into battle, Reuben's sons are portrayed as hanging back while they "search their hearts." Skeptics interpret this ambivalence as just an excuse not to go to war as they should.

I don't think this lukewarm reputation may be deserved for two reasons. First, the Reubenite men did their part in fighting battles to help their brothers and sisters take the Promised Land, and the Bible makes that very clear. Only after they fulfilled their responsibilities did they return to their land in Gilead. Second, the choice to settle in Gilead may have been part of God's strategy to help the Israelites in later battles.

Finally, while there is no evidence that Reuben can be held personally accountable for passing on this trait to his clan, we know that our actions can have a profound influence on our children and beyond. Although God can redeem us and our circumstances, our sinful words and actions may set an example we will regret for our children and their children, our nieces and nephews, our neighbors, and even our siblings. Sin is never acceptable even for our own sakes, but knowing children are looking to us to model how to live makes our sins doubly repellent to us. Because of the children in our lives (our own and those in our community) we should take to heart Thessalonians 5:22:

22 *Abstain from every form of evil.*

The King James Version says to *"abstain from all appearance of evil."* We should walk a wide circle around choices, situations, places, and events that can damage our witness to the unsaved and those younger or weaker in their walks.

GRACE POINT: To me, there is no finer example of men standing by their word than when the sons of Reuben went away to battle and fought the battles of the other tribes in order to settle the Promised Land and clear out the enemies there. They valiantly helped Joshua fight to settle Canaan (Joshua 22:1-4.) They could have said, "Wait until we settle our new lands and get our families protected," but they did not. Again, we see honor and integrity in the way they fought enemies that were no longer their own. To me, I think Reuben's family, though flawed like all families, was redeemed.

What about you? Has God allowed some consequences of your actions to affect you or those around you? Have you seen His Grace in it yet? Are you praying for it?

In Reuben's life, I see heinous, infamous sin, but more than that I see Grace upon Grace. Grace abounding. Grace that is greater than Reuben's sin or mine. Praise the Lord!

DEVOTIONAL 14: WHEN YOUR PRAYER LIFE FEELS BARREN

At a later time, I will devote several weeks to the topic of prayer, but I feel it is important to share now something God showed me recently. You see, I have been contacted by so many people lately who feel they are not hearing from God regarding an issue they have long prayed about, and He did something recently that encouraged me deeply about praying without seeing evidence of results. I am writing this in February. This has been a month of brutal cold, interspersed with a rare day here and there in the 60s and 70s.

One day last week, I stopped to soak in the beautiful sunlight pouring through my second floor bedroom windows. It had been so cold and dark for weeks, but this day was springlike and lovely. I walked over to my bank of windows and looked out. Down below me, I saw the top of a tree I normally see from the ground view. I usually see this tree as I am walking on the sidewalk and am looking up. The tree has been very bare and stark all winter, and especially this week. But today, I was looking from a different vantage point, far above the tree and looking down. I saw something unusual at the very top of the branches that I could not identify. At first, I thought it was snow on the very tips of the top branches. But it was not the cold and icy snow of winter- this tree was budding in the dead of winter!

All across the tips of the branches at the very crown of the tree were tiny green leaves and emerging white buds creating a lacy pattern that could be seen only when looking down. The branches below looked like dry sticks, barren of any sign of life. Only at the very tip top ends of the uppermost branches closest to the sun could any sign of new life be seen.

Our prayer life is like that. We are earth bound. We have a limited view of our circumstances because of our earthly vantage point. We pray for things, and it appears that nothing happens. But things **ARE** happening. Far above us and far beyond us on God's timeline, things are happening—and it is good. We rarely get the glimpse of the new hope and growth budding in our lives in advance, just as I saw the tops of the trees budding this week *for the first time in the fifteen years* I have lived here. We are not entitled to know the end from the beginning. That belongs to God:

remember the former things of old;
for I am God, and there is no other;
*   I am God, and there is none like me,*
10 *declaring the end from the beginning*
*   and from ancient times things not yet done,*
saying, 'My counsel shall stand,
*   and I will accomplish all my purpose,'*
11 *calling a bird of prey from the east,*
*   the man of my counsel from a far country.*
I have spoken, and I will bring it to pass;
*   I have purposed, and I will do it. Isaiah 46:9-11 **

God sees yesterday, today and tomorrow. We do not have the tomorrow viewpoint. We cannot always get above our circumstances and look down and get the God perspective. But we can try every day to see the circumstances of our lives and events through His eyes. Only He can see the future, but through prayer and soaking daily in His words, we can begin to think more and more like Him and to see things more as He sees them.

One of my privileges is to pray with young women who are active in various programs for the 20s and 30s age group at our church or whom I knew when teaching at Georgia State University. Praying with some of them for many years has allowed me to see their disappointments as well as their joys. We have prayed together over many broken hearts and lost loves. At times, the seemingly perfect young man has not been ready for marriage or the young woman has felt the Holy Spirit prompting her to move on, even though she wanted to stay. But then God sends her husband, the right young man not just for her 20s and 30s but for her 40s, 60s, and 80s! This choice is so right that I usually cannot stop myself from saying, "Aren't you glad God made you wait? Is this not the perfect person for you?" (Yes, I am that person who will actually say that!) Oh, the joy on their faces as they clearly show that God blessed them when He deprived them of what they thought they wanted.

God has seen the end from the beginning! He knows the exactly right answer to your prayers. He always answers prayers; it's just that His timing and His answers are not always earthbound like ours. His are so much higher and better for our futures.

I don't want to make light of how hard it is when you have prayed for something for years, and you do not see the answer you are seeking. But make no mistake, God is actively answering that prayer right now. He may be preparing the perfect outcome. He may be changing <u>you</u> as you labor in prayer and grow in trust and submission. I cannot tell you what God is doing, but I can tell you He is not idle or unresponsive. Your prayers are not barren. They will result in fruit. Your hope is valid. Something new is budding in you or in God's plan; all may look bone dry and dead from where you stand right now, but God is actively working in your life and in the lives of others He will send across your path. He sees the new growth, the green of emerging hope, and things that will blossom later that only He can see.

*You will sometimes see me quote a passage where God is talking to someone specifically, usually the people of Israel. Although some of these passages were not written to you about your circumstances, I think they are instructive about how God has handled similar situations in the past. Part of getting to know anyone, even God, is learning about their character and nature, and reading about God's dealings with others teaches us those things. These passages are particularly valuable when God shares how He looks at His authority or His relationships with His children of other eras. Since He is unchanging in His love and constant in His principles, I think sharing these words written to others can help us understand how He might be looking at our circumstances.

DEVOTIONAL 15: PREPARING YOUR HEART FOR EASTER - CONFESSION & REPENTANCE

As we approach the Holy days of Good Friday and Easter, are you being prompted to prepare your heart for the beauty and grief of these events in our Savior's life? This is a celebration of the miracle of Resurrection that paid for our sin forever and ever when He said, "It is finished," but the cost was great. Through His choice to pay the penalty of death to cancel our sin, we can now go to the Father's throne sinless and clean; but we cannot forget the unthinkable price Jesus had to pay for our sins. My individual sins. Your individual sins. You and I caused the thorns, the piercings, the nails, and the cross.

Because of our part in sending Jesus to that cross, we should take a moment to think deeply about two things we should do every day of our lives, but especially Easter: confession and repentance.

Confession has two meanings in the Bible. Sometimes we are told to confess the Lord Jesus and tell about Him. Paul did this when he appeared as a prisoner in front of King Agrippa and shocked the people who feared for him by saying boldly to the king:

25 ... "I am not out of my mind, most excellent Festus, but I am speaking true and rational words. 26 For the king knows about these things, and to him I speak boldly. For I am persuaded that none of these things has escaped his notice, for this has not been done in a corner. 27 King Agrippa, do you believe the prophets? I know that you believe." 28 And Agrippa said to Paul, "In a short time would you persuade me to be a Christian?" 29 And Paul said, "Whether short or long, I would to God that not only you but also all who hear me this day might become such as I am—except for these chains." Acts 26: 25-29

Throughout that chapter (Acts 26), Paul does what many Christians with an effective witness do: he told the nonbelievers how Jesus acted in his life that led to his conversion and gained him the *"help that comes from God."*

But today we are focusing on the other type of confession, the type of confession that leads to repentance. Christians are commanded to confess throughout the Old Testament and the New. I John 1:9 says:

9 If we confess our sins, he is faithful and just to forgive us our sins and to cleanse us from all unrighteousness.

So confession is foundational to forgiveness and cleansing, and we all want and need forgiveness and cleansing.

But how do we do this in the 21st century church? The rules and regulations are quite clear in the church under the law in the Old Testament, but now that Jesus has freed us from the law, what does confession look like?

Confession starts with private confession. Many wonderful Christians who give their time, effort, and passion to serving the Lord constantly actually have the hardest time with private confession. They try so hard to avoid sin and they are scrupulous in studying the Bible so they don't put themselves in situations that may lead to sin. They so don't want to sin that they almost cannot bear to think that a thought they may have or a conversation or action is just as sinful as the blatantly sinful people around them. In comparison to others, they feel they are not leading a sinful life. They may actually not see sins of a critical spirit, gossip, lack of discipline, self-congratulation, or intemperance. I remember almost thirty years ago, being in a Bible study with a woman considered a pillar of her church. She had given her children a Biblically sound upbringing, and one had become a missionary. But one day, the anger in her heart came pouring out when she said, "I was never wild as a teenager. I always obeyed my parents. I watched while others around me in my twenties and thirties drank and partied and sowed their wild oats. Then they up and come to the Lord after having all that fun, and they are considered just as sinless as I am. I don't think that is right."

But that is how Grace works. I thank God daily we do not get what we deserve.

One meaning of "confess" is to acknowledge. We must first acknowledge that we have sinned before the repentance can start.

Seeing our sin is extremely difficult when we feel justified in our choices. That is why having a prayer partner or an accountability group is vital to the mature Christian. Confession does not have to be in front of the entire church or to a pastor. You need Christians around you who care enough about your maintaining a close relationship with the Lord that they will tell you when the motives of your heart are questionable or when the words you chose could have been kinder or when your discipline is eroding in an area. I have prayer partners who are very much like me, but I also have prayer partners who are very different from me and may even make me uncomfortable, because they can see my biases, my slips, and my sin faster and better than those who see everything through a filter of our friendship.

Repentance should swiftly follow confession. 2 Corinthians 7:10 says that *"Godly grief produces a repentance that leads to salvation without regret, whereas worldly grief produces death."* We should not just say, "Yes, I sinned," but we should grieve over our sin and allow the Lord to change us and save us. That is my prayer almost every morning after I confess: "Lord, change me. Don't leave me this way. Through you, help me to be different in the next situation. Make me more like you."

So after confessing, your repentance should result in some kind of change. You may not be perfect after repenting, but you should be heading in a different direction with the Lord's help. Sometimes we are stumbling at first, but if we persist in prayer, He will set our course in a Godly direction.

Honestly, there are many people who are uncomfortable with the confessions and repentance I have talked about in this blog and when I speak at events. One reason I share my failings is that there are people I love who are struggling with confession and repentance, many who have led Godly lives for decades. Another reason I confess publicly is that privately I have received emails telling me that these confessions have helped women because they were really having trouble with that part of prayer. To those readers, I say, "Be encouraged, dear sisters, if you are reading this today. The very fact that you know you are in a battle means you have taken the most important step towards repentance- admitting you need to confess and that you are struggling."

Many years ago, a pastor said he saw no need for repentance because he was no longer a sinner and that Christ has taken care of all repentance at the time of salvation. The purifying and cleansing work is a done deal, but let me share some of the reasons Christians still need to confess and repent.

1. So that you can be healed

Repentance is a prerequisite to being healed of our sin sick nature as well as physical healing from the Lord.

Therefore, confess your sins to one another and pray for one another, that you may be healed. The prayer of a righteous person has great power as it is working. James 5:16

2. So that God can do great things through you and your life can bear fruit

8 Bear fruits in keeping with repentance. And do not begin to say to yourselves, 'We have Abraham as our father.' Luke 3:8

Before great men of God accomplished historically consequential things for the Lord, you will usually see that they spent time in confession and repentance. Ezra personally confesses in Ezra 9 and then leads the people in public repentance in chapter 10 as they repopulate Jerusalem.

1 While Ezra prayed and made confession, weeping and casting himself down before the house of God, a very great assembly of men, women, and children, gathered to him out of Israel, for the people wept bitterly. 2 And Shecaniah the son of Jehiel, of the sons of Elam, addressed Ezra: "We have broken faith with our God and have married foreign women from the peoples of the land, but even now there is hope for Israel in spite of this… 11 Now then make confession to the Lord, the God of your fathers and do his will. Ezra 10:1-2, 11

In Nehemiah 9, the prophet models for us how critical confession is when we pray for the impossible through the Lord's power and mercy. For a full quarter of the day, he leads Israel in confession and worship.

The building of the wall was a feat that was humanly impossible, but Nehemiah was able to get an unbelieving king to fund the entire project!

1 Now on the twenty-fourth day of this month the people of Israel were assembled with fasting and in sackcloth, and with earth on their heads.2 And the Israelites separated themselves from all foreigners and stood and confessed their sins and the iniquities of their fathers. 3 And they stood up in their place and read from the Book of the Law of the Lord their God for a quarter of the day; for another quarter of it they made confession and worshiped the Lord their God. Nehemiah 9:1-3

3. Because Christians still sin

Paul is addressing believers in the church when in 2 Corinthians 12:21 he predicts he may have to mourn over those who have sinned and "not repented."

1 I fear that when I come again my God may humble me before you, and I may have to mourn over many of those who sinned earlier and have not repented of the impurity, sexual immorality, and sensuality that they have practiced. 2 Corinthians 12:21

4. So that you can be saved and receive life and the Holy Spirit

Peter, Paul, and other disciples clearly told believers the value of repentance.

38 And Peter said to them, "Repent and be baptized every one of you in the name of Jesus Christ for the forgiveness of your sins, and you will receive the gift of the Holy Spirit. Acts 2:38

5. Because Jesus said so

Shortly after John the Baptist dies, Christ officially begins his public ministry. In Matthew's account of Jesus' earliest preaching, the first recorded words Jesus said addressed repentance:

17 From that time Jesus began to preach, saying,"'Repent, for the kingdom of heaven is at   hand.' " Matthew 4:17

Matthew also underscores the high value God places on repentance by referencing some of the most infamously sinful people the world has ever known, the citizens of Nineveh. Matthew 12 says these ungodly people will have the right to condemn the current generation because the Ninevites repented when Jonah preached. People today have Jesus' teaching and preaching to guide them:

41 The men of Nineveh will rise up at the judgment with this generation and condemn it, for they repented at the preaching of Jonah, and behold, something greater than Jonah is here. Matthew 12:41

Consider how confession and repentance play a role in your relationship with Jesus Christ. Do you intentionally examine your heart, your days, and your relationships to be sure you are confessing subtle sins? Do you have prayer partners who will help you see when sin starts to creep into your life?

Before Easter comes, please consider having a special time of confession and repentance to prepare your heart to rejoice. Yes, your sins are forgiven and the price has been paid forever, so be sure you are ready to fully celebrate with nothing between Him and you that has not been confessed.

DEVOTIONAL 16: SPRING!

I am puzzled how people can be agnostics or atheists at two particular times in life. One is at the birth of a child into one's family. The minute the baby is born, you can see the detail of a complete human being is all there. Looking at those baby fingers with their perfectly etched lines on the knuckles and the complete and unique fingerprints, to me, makes an irrefutable case that there is a Designer and a Creator behind His creation. The detail of His design boggles my mind, especially because I know we are made in His image and are like our Father just as you can often see a baby's father in his features or the way he moves or laughs. It is miraculous when you see a parent's jaw or forehead or some other feature, perfectly replicated in a newborn. How does God do that? Surely, you cannot still believe this is an accident?

The second time that defies disbelief to me is spring in the south. In my hometown outside Atlanta, just stepping out the door confronts you with beauty in every direction: the dogwoods, cherry blossoms, crepe myrtles, azaleas, all are blossoming profusely and make my heart leap for joy. Thank you, God!

On closer look, each petal and stamen is different. Looking into the heart of any flower reveals the Creator who has painted this world with color and beauty that no artist can compete with. The fine touches are breathtaking.

What does this tell us about God? How are we like Him since we are made in His image? First of all, we know that He loves beauty and that He loves to delight us. We know this because He shows it by His actions and attention to detail. We know this because He gave us the senses to enjoy His handiwork. Thank you, God!

He tells us to stay our minds on things that are lovely. *"Finally, brothers, whatever is true, whatever is honorable, whatever is just, whatever is pure, whatever is lovely, whatever is commendable, if* there is any excellence, if there is anything worthy of praise, think about these things." Philippians 4:8

We also know God because He speaks to us through people who knew Him well. He gave His thoughts, observations, and laws to those who experienced Him in a very personal way- prophets, poets, kings, apostles, and others. He talked to them. He allowed them to witness how He worked out impossible situations and at times dazzled them with demonstrations of His power. His words through them are collected in the Bible, and in reading it, you hear His thoughts on spring. .

He feels very much like we do when we walk out our door in the springtime. Here is what He inspired one of his prophets to write:

"The desert and the parched land will be glad; the wilderness will rejoice and blossom. Like the crocus, it will burst into bloom; it will rejoice greatly and shout for joy. The glory of Lebanon will be given to it, the splendor of Carmel and Sharon; they will see the glory of the LORD, the splendor of our God." Isaiah 35:1-2

He inspired one writer to compare our worldwide church to a bride that He is accompanying on a spring walk after the dark of winter:

"My beloved spoke and said to me, "Arise, my darling, my beautiful one, come with me.

See! The winter is past; the rains are over and gone. Flowers appear on the earth; the season of singing has come, the cooing of doves is heard in our land. The fig tree forms its early fruit; the blossoming vines spread their fragrance. Arise, come, my darling; my beautiful one, come with me." Song of Solomon 2:10-13

And Matthew 6:28-29 reveals that His artistry in the detail of the lily is very intentional, that He has dressed them with care:

"And why do you worry about clothes? See how the flowers of the field grow. They do not labor or spin. Yet I tell you that not even Solomon in all his splendor was dressed like one of these."

I used to believe that the reason the South was called the Bible Belt and had so many Christians was because of all of His glory demonstrated around us through His creation. I believed it was just easier for us to believe. How can we deny it with such profuse evidence everywhere we look? But people in Arizona and New Mexico feel that about the gold and purple hues of the desert. My friend from Montana leaves the robust beauty of the South each year because she cannot wait to get to the place whose beauty moves her more, Montana. I remember being staggered by my awareness of God the first time I stood at the foot of the Rocky Mountains. His works make a statement.

Wherever you live, pause a moment to see what God has done around you recently. Walk outside and ask God to allow you to see things the way He does. Remember that His impulse is to make things beautiful and to fill minds and senses with lovely things. All of this is for your mutual joy and sharing. Contemplate that you are made in His image. Like the flowers and trees, you have been "endowed by the Creator" (from Declaration of Independence, Thomas Jefferson) and placed in this world primarily for His delight. Just as a flower delights Him just by being where God placed it, so we delight Him just by being where He wants us to be in relation to Him. Our fellowship and proximity to Him are by far our highest priority.

Take a moment or an hour this week to just enjoy Him and to thank Him that He created you uniquely for His enjoyment and fellowship with you, His most loved creation. He loves being with you and seeing you, His creation, grow through all your various stages, even the costly dark ones. Take an intentional moment this week to enjoy the works of His hands and allow yourself to know that He is enjoying His creations, too, even (and maybe especially) you.

DEVOTIONAL 17: MAIS OUI!

By now you may have figured out that I have two guilty pleasures. One is that after a period of intense writing when I barely leave my home for weeks except to go to church or after the opposite kind of busy time of being with people constantly when I speak, this introvert likes to steal away, take the Sunday newspaper, and have a long slow leisurely meal in absolute solitude. The other is that I am an incurable eavesdropper. Being alone in restaurants in my travels has made me privy to some very interesting conversations.

This Saturday, one of those rare opportunities presented itself. I had been so rushed all day that I had not eaten. I found myself at 1:00PM on a different side of town but very near a buffet that had items that were perfect for my persnickety diet plan, so I grabbed the Sunday paper (still unopened from the previous Sunday) and found a quiet table.

It was not quiet for long. The woman sitting behind me decided to have a long conversation with what must have been her closest friend. The cell phone call that was still going on after an hour when I left was so loud that I could not help hearing every word. (Don't judge me:)

But don't worry, I did not intrude on this woman's privacy because the entire conversation was in French! The woman was deeply and energetically enjoying the heartfelt communication with the person on the other end. The honeyed, dulcet tones from time to time held love for her friend. She laughed, exclaimed, sympathized, and seemed to be appropriately outraged when her friend told her of some injustice.

But what struck me was that every sentence seemed to be punctuated with "mais oui (pronounced may-wee)." Sometimes she would say it excitedly twice in one sentence, "Mais oui! Mais oui!" I had to find out what this phrase meant because it seemed the perfect thing to say to a friend when you are listening with all your heart, responding with passion and love, and wanting to support her with all that is in you.

Reverso.net and Colliers revealed that "mais oui" can mean, "but, yes," "why, yes," "exactly," and "but, of course." In other words, this phrase always means affirmation. It seems to be a very emphatic agreement and not just the bland "ah" and "I see" I have been giving my friends. It seems more to say, "Yes, I see it exactly as you see it, and I could not agree with you more!" "Yes, I am just as enthusiastic about hearing your news as you are to tell it!" "Yes, you were completely right in that situation and I applaud your actions." "Yes, I have always thought that and looked at it exactly that way." Now *that* is the way to respond to a friend.

I drove away thinking of my friends who have been that woman in my life to say "Mais oui" to all I undertake or aspire to. The ones who threw me a luncheon and gave me a very special crystal objet d'art by a local artist to commemorate the sale of my first book before we ever knew it would sell. To them, it was already a hit because it was from me!

The ones who take my part when the world tells me I am wrong. The ones who prayed with me when I tried to figure out if I were setting too strong a boundary or being co-dependent; I just felt wrong either way, but they knew my heart and knew God saw my desire to only be in His will. The ones whom I call because there is no one else who lives in my house with me now, and they always take my call and listen to the funny things that happened that day or the little hurts or the blessings God continues to give me. The ones I can talk to without a filter and not be judged as we grab that rare hour alone together. They are the ones I do not have to explain that the tiny miracle that happened on my lunch hour was a love touch from God; the minute I tell them, they start praising with me and NEVER suggest it was a coincidence. They are the ones that when I grapple with trying to express the nuance of a moment that was beautiful or uncomfortable or breathtaking and cannot find the words, say, "I know exactly what you mean."

Everything in my life to them is a "mais oui."

God wanted to be that person in our lives to help us, affirm us, and support us through the inevitable hardships He knew we would face in our time on earth. He understands us in the deepest way that even our closest friends cannot grasp. He knows us in our souls and our minds. He knows our past, present, and future. He sent Jesus Christ to communicate with us in the deepest way His love and that He is *for* us. Jesus came to be the connection to the Father that our sin-covered souls could never make happen without help.

In 2 Corinthians 1:19-20, Paul is explaining who God is and says, *"For the Son of God, Jesus Christ, whom we proclaimed among you, Silvanus and Timothy and I, was not Yes and No, but in him it is always Yes. For all the promises of God find their Yes in him. That is why it is through him that we utter our Amen to God for his glory."*

This is why Jesus came, to fulfill every promise of the Father to you personally from Genesis to Revelation, and there are many. He also came to establish sweet communion with the Father, an ongoing conversation with your closest friend. Because of Him, God is always available to you 24/7 to hear your joys, your pain, your confusion. He will not tell you that you are right when you are wrong, but right or wrong, He will affirm that you are His child and that He is **for** you. And He has told you that all of His plans are to bless you, so He is always on your side- never doubt it (Romans 8:28, Jeremiah 29:11.) He is the greatest "Mais oui" person in your life.

If you have never asked Him into your life, I hope you will today. Mais oui! Mais oui!

DEVOTIONAL 18: WHEN YOU SEE HIS FACE

There is a moment in my future that I anticipate with so much delight that I cannot express how wonderful it is. I can barely contain my excitement when I allow myself to think about it. It is more thrilling than any earthly moment I have ever looked forward to, even when I was a child and wildly anticipated Christmas and other events. This moment is unimaginable because there is nothing earthly to compare it to. It is the moment I first open my eyes in Heaven, and Jesus and I are gazing directly into each other's faces.

I rarely allow myself the luxury of letting this excitement move me this way. I became committed long ago not to view my Christianity as a down payment on Heaven. I don't live for the rewards (though I don't deny them.) I so want to obey Him simply because I love Him that I shy away from dwelling on the glory and joy and spectacle of living eternally with Him in Heaven, but that is a part of my future I can bank on. Today, I felt God encouraging me to thrill to the anticipation of what comes next for me after I die.

I have just come from our Easter services that focused on the **empty** cross and the message of Resurrection. In his awe-inspiring prayer, our friend Tom alluded to the moment when Jesus appeared to Mary Magdalene just after He had risen. She was going about her morning (Mark 16:2) when she turned and there was Jesus (verse 9)! She is so stunned that she cannot comprehend this is Jesus, but then He speaks her name and she knows (John 20:16).

I have that moment in my future, and if you have asked Him into your life, so do you. Do you find that as thrilling as I do? I think I will feel such relief and think, "At last, at last. I see my Savior face-to-face." That relief was echoed when our musicians sang these words by Jeremy Camp:

There will be a day with no more tears,
No more pain, and no more fears

There will be a day when the burdens of this place
Will be no more, we'll see Jesus face to face.[1]

The next song focused me even more on that day that I have anticipated for years yet that I will have no inkling of until it arrives— the day that I will turn, and there He will be. We will look into each other's faces knowing each other honestly and being fully known, both of our faces full of so much mutual love. Oh, the joy! Oh, the excitement of the fulfillment of a long-awaited and long anticipated moment! His face! I will see His face!

The Gaither song describes that day this way:

And then one day, I'll cross that river
I'll fight life's final war with pain
And then, as death gives way to vict'ry
I'll see the lights of glory and I'll know He reigns.[2]

And that day is coming for me— an incomparable moment to look forward to daily as I walk with Him in a different way now on earth.

I have sometimes gotten a sense of this after losing a dear friend or family member. Because we are absent from the body and then present with the Lord, I know where my Christian friends are as soon as that last breath leaves their bodies. In the midst of my sadness and loss, I know deeply that they are experiencing a joy in that moment that I cannot comprehend, and I am happy for them. But today I am selfishly thinking about *my* moment, my first moment when I will not have the barriers I have now to just sitting and looking Jesus "full in His wonderful face" (Helen Lemmel).[3]

If you are unsure of what you will experience one minute after you die, please contact me at Christianityadventures@gmail.com. I would love for you to know what is deservedly called "the greatest joy."

Easter blessings on my brothers and sisters who are celebrating with me in this season of Resurrection. And blessings and good tidings of great joy to you if you do not know Jesus personally. Reading this today is just one part of what God is doing to reveal Himself to you one-on-one. Keep your heart and mind open to what He is trying to say to you so that one day you will have the thrill of seeing Him face-to-face.

Reading from the Bible:

The Gospel According to John

1. "There Will Be a Day" as written by Jeremy Camp. Lyrics © CAPITOL CHRISTIAN MUSIC GROUP

2. .Because He Lives lyrics as written by Gloria Gaither and William J. Gaither © CAPITOL CHRISTIAN MUSIC GROUP

3. Turn Your Eyes Upon Jesus as written by Helen Lemmel. Timelesstruths.org

DEVOTIONAL 19: LORD, DON'T YOU CARE THAT WE ARE PERISHING?

Have you ever felt like crying out to God because He seemed to be asleep at the wheel of your life? Have you ever felt He surely could not be tuned in to what is going on with you because you were hurting or terrified or heartbroken? Then you are like those closest to Him, his disciples, when they called out to Him, *" 'Teacher, do you not care that we are perishing?' "* In Mark 4:38-41, when a terrible storm comes up suddenly and their ship is in danger, a few of his disciples are afraid for their lives. They cry out plaintively to the Lord because He has fallen asleep, seemingly unconcerned about what is happening to them.

One of my dearest friends lost her daughter this week. Monica, at age 48 went home to live with Jesus in Heaven for eternity. She fought one of the most difficult battles with cancer that I have ever witnessed. This beautiful masterpiece of a woman was what we all aspire to be as Christian women. She lived for the Lord every day of her life and her cancer years and death were an even greater testimony of her faith than her years of health. The joy of the Lord shined on her countenance despite debilitating chemo treatments. She was clearly at peace, though she received one devastating report from her doctor after another for years. In the world's eyes, there was no happy ending. But they don't see the ending.

Just one of the many passages that comforts Christians is 2 Corinthians 5.

5 For we know that if the tent that is our earthly home is destroyed, we have a building from God, a house not made with hands, eternal in the heavens. 2 For in this tent we groan, longing to put on our heavenly dwelling, 3 if indeed by putting it on we may not be found naked. 4 For while we are still in this tent, we groan, being burdened—not that we would be unclothed, but that we would be further clothed, so that what is mortal may be swallowed up by life. 5 He who has prepared us for this very thing is God, who has given us the Spirit as a guarantee.

6 So we are always of good courage. We know that while we are at home in the body we are away from the Lord, 7 for we walk by faith, not by sight. 8 Yes, we are of good courage, and we would rather be away from the body and at home with the Lord. 9 So whether we are at home or away, we make it our aim to please him. 10 For we must all appear before the judgment seat of Christ, so that each one may receive what is due for what he has done in the body, whether good or evil.

Here are three things I take from this passage.

1.   The moment Monica finished her difficult journey here on earth, folded her earthly tent, and left this world and took the hand of Jesus, she was absent from her body but present with the Lord. The incredibly wonderful Christians I have known who went to Heaven before I wanted them to have this one thing in common: because I know how they loved Jesus with all their hearts, I know they would not step back into this life even if they could. The healing I wanted for them is nothing compared to how wonderful they are feeling in His presence. And we will enjoy that with them one day and for eternity. This waiting time seems long to us, but one day we will see it is just the blink of an eye. So Monica would say to us, *"Yes, we are of good courage, and we would rather be away from the body and at home with the Lord."* (Verse 8.)

2.   Monica experienced much pain and sickness while on this earth. We all do to some degree, but hers was extensive. Verse 4 says, "For while we are still in this tent, we groan, being burdened." Monica is no longer groaning. She is experiencing something you have never had a moment of: the experience of having not a single burden in the world. She has a wholeness we can't even grasp; her relationships are perfect; she rests completely in God's provision and care; and she enjoys worship and fellowship with Him like none she has ever known.

3.   Verse 10 says, *"For we must all appear before the judgment seat of Christ, so that each one may receive what is due for what he has done in the body, whether good or evil."* Monica's main credential is that she took the Lord at His Word and asked Him to live in her heart and save her from her sinful self and accepted His salvation. That one choice made the difference in what happened to Monica the moment life left her body. The bliss and joy she experiences every

minute is entirely dependent on that day she said, "Yes, I choose to believe you," to the Lord. But in addition to that, Monica served Him on this earth, taught others about the Lord, went on mission trips to ensure others far away could know His love, and set an example for me and others about how our lives should look after we accept Jesus. She was a Godly woman in the eyes of every single person who ever met her. She had nothing to fear at the judgment seat.

Monica has her happy ending, a happiness so great the world cannot begin to create anything remotely similar. This world could not offer someone as wonderful as Monica the joy and delight she is enjoying now. In the old days, people would have said, "She has gone to her reward." That is exactly what has happened. God used Monica's life and her process of death to bring Him glory while she was with us, but now, she is enjoying her reward. I am praising the Lord for that as I pray for comfort for her family who have lost a remarkable person.

Jesus came to bind up the brokenhearted. I am praying that Monica's husband, mother, brothers, and other family members feel His loving touch as He binds up their wounded hearts. I pray they will be more aware than ever of the Comforter, the Holy Spirit. And I am praying that they will be able to experience the joy of knowing that they will be living with her in glory for many more years than they had with her on earth and enjoying the Lord with her forever. I know the Lord will carry them in His loving arms through this pain.

The Lord was not asleep when Monica died. He brought her to live with Him for eternity. Everything in her life was used as a blessing, though our limited understanding cannot fathom all of it now.

And He is not asleep in your circumstances. When Jesus rebuked the wind and calmed the storm the disciples were in, they were stunned. They said, *"Who then is this, that even the wind and the sea obey him?"* It is our Lord, the Master over everything. The Master over whatever has your heart hurting or faltering. Doesn't He care? Yes, He cares so much He died an even worse death than we can imagine to take your place and pay for your sins. And He can rebuke and change whatever is stirring in your life if you ask Him to. Just because you do not hear Him for a while does not mean He is asleep. Trust His character. Trust what He has told you from His Word. He will be there for you in life and He will be there for you in death.

(Today's story from Mark 4:35-41 is printed below for you. How might it apply to something in your life?)

35 On that day, when evening had come, he said to them, "Let us go across to the other side." 36 And leaving the crowd, they took him with them in the boat, just as he was. And other boats were with him. 37 And a great windstorm arose, and the waves were breaking into the boat, so that the boat was already filling. 38 But he was in the stern, asleep on the cushion. And they woke him and said to him, "Teacher, do you not care that we are perishing?" 39 And he awoke and rebuked the wind and said to the sea, "Peace! Be still!" And the wind ceased, and there was a great calm. 40 He said to them, "Why are you so afraid? Have you still no faith?" 41 And they were filled with great fear and said to one another, "Who then is this, that even the wind and the sea obey him?"

DEVOTIONAL 20: MARY, MOTHER OF JESUS: CALLED TO BE DIFFERENT

God calls us to such different lives. It is easy to see the life that God has called some people to such as Anne Graham Lotz or Elisabeth Elliot. We see how He placed them exactly in the geographic location, the family, the marriage, or the ministry they were supposed to experience in order to reflect His glory. It is more difficult to see that He has done exactly that for you and for me. Our day-to-day life events are so in our faces that they obscure the fact that God has placed us here to be reflectors of His Grace, love, and salvation.

Mary, the mother of Jesus, was given one of the most difficult paths. For a young Jewish girl, being found with child that was not the child of one's betrothed was one of those "end of the world" experiences young girls fear. More than that, Mary could have been stoned for it. But although Mary did not fully understand the particulars of her new circumstance, from the moment the angel told her she was to give birth to the Savior, she embraced her new assignment, though there were potentially dangerous unknowns and great difficulty ahead. This is the dialogue with the angel as she receives the news:

And the virgin's name was Mary.28 And he came to her and said, "Greetings, O favoured one, the Lord is with you!" 29 But she was greatly troubled at the saying, and tried to discern what sort of greeting this might be. 30 And the angel said to her, "Do not be afraid, Mary, for you have found favour with God. 31 And behold, you will conceive in your womb and bear a son, and you shall call his name Jesus. 32 He will be great and will be called the Son of the Most High. And the Lord God will give to him the throne of his father David, 33 and he will reign over the house of Jacob for ever, and of his kingdom there will be no end."34 And Mary said to the angel, "How will this be, since I am a virgin?" 35 And the angel answered her, "The Holy Spirit will come upon you, and the power of the Most High will overshadow you; therefore the child to be born will be called holy—the Son of God. 36 And behold, your relative Elizabeth in her old age has also conceived a son, and this is the sixth month with her who was called barren. 37 For nothing will be impossible with God." 38 And

Mary said, "Behold, I am the servant of the Lord; let it be to me according to your word." And the angel departed from her.

And Mary did not just accept, she praised God in her difficult and confusing circumstances. Though her life was totally out of control and would bring public condemnation on her, she was bursting with joy and gratitude because this what God had chosen for her:

46 *And Mary said,*
"My soul magnifies the Lord,
47   *and my spirit rejoices in God my Saviour,*
48 *for he has looked on the humble estate of his servant.*
   For behold, from now on all generations will call me blessed;
49 *for he who is mighty has done great things for me,*
   and holy is his name.
50 *And his mercy is for those who fear him*
   from generation to generation.
51 *He has shown strength with his arm;*
   he has scattered the proud in the thoughts of their hearts;
52 *he has brought down the mighty from their thrones·*
   and exalted those of humble estate;
53 *he has filled the hungry with good things,*
   and the rich he has sent away empty.
54 *He has helped his servant Israel,*
   in remembrance of his mercy,
55 *as he spoke to our fathers,*
   to Abraham and to his offspring forever." Luke 1:46-55

Is there perhaps a circumstance in your life that seems to be difficult or burdensome? Could it be that it is in the midst of this dark and unwanted circumstance that God can use you to shine brightly as you reflect His glory? Can you walk through a circumstance that is the last thing you would have planned for your life and do it in a way that reflects the radiance of Jesus Christ in you? The darkest context of a life best reveals the way Jesus can shine through. For Elisabeth Elliot, it was the violent death of her beloved husband Jim. Anne Graham Lotz honed her personal joy and zest for the Lord amid the monotony and confinement of staying home for years with young children. Mary was asked to stand and watch as her beloved oldest child was tortured and crucified.

Where God has placed you is no accident. Talk to Him today about your circumstances. Have a Mary conversation with Him. Ask Him to help you shine in whatever place you are and through whatever He has in store for you in your future. Then trust Him to do His work through you because you are willing. Ask Him to shine brightly even if you feel your circumstances are dark or clouded with confusion or doubts. The darker the circumstances the brighter His light can shine to others around you.

DEVOTIONAL 21: WOMEN LIVING FOR JESUS

The New Testament is full of references to the female followers of Jesus. In a culture that often did not mention women's names or did not even count them fully as people, the fact that the Bible names them attests to their importance to Jesus. Sometimes these women became devoted to serving the Lord and contributing to His ministry after He healed them of an illness or delivered them from an evil spirit. Joanna, the wife of Chuza, Herod's household manager, and Susanna were two of these women, and they did much to support Jesus' early ministry and that of the Apostles. Joanna is later mentioned again as one of the women who brought spices to anoint the body of Jesus, only to find He had risen. Also present that day was Salome, who had also been with Mary at the Crucifixion. (Mark 16:1, 15:40, Luke 24:10.)

These are not perfect women. Salome who was honored to be part of Mary's inner circle (and was perhaps her half-sister.) She was almost certainly the one (Mary Salome) who asked Jesus to show favoritism to her sons, James and John, in Matthew 20:20-22b:

20 Then came to him the mother of Zebedee's children with her sons, worshipping him, and desiring a certain thing of him.

21 And he said unto her, What wilt thou? She saith unto him, Grant that these my two sons may sit, the one on thy right hand, and the other on the left, in thy kingdom.

22 But Jesus answered and said, Ye know not what ye ask.

These are women with flaws and pasts and sin struggles. But they are women who will show up when the Lord makes them aware of a need. They are women who will come alongside the grieving and be with them as they bury their family members. They are women who will contribute their time and money to their church to the extent they possibly can. They will be there serving to help feed God's people as well as the poor outside the walls of the church, just because they know this is what Jesus wants. And they work behind the scenes, often going nameless as others are recognized.

My church is full of these women who do not receive accolades or recognition as they week in and week out, year in and year out, consistently serve with all that is in them.

I think of Anne who writes lovely notes to some of the sick and grieving people in our church who are on our prayer list and who have supplied their contact information. I see her going alone into our prayer room weekly to pour over the requests to see who has indicated that a note would be welcome. And she writes those from her sweet heart as guided by the Holy Spirit.

Wanzie makes sure that she has prayed over every prayer request from our Sunday service. She and her sister Elizabeth are such cheerful but quiet additions to any group they attend and are faithful and bold to witness in their apartment complex.

Linda and Joyce serve in so many "spots" where help is needed that I won't mention them all. From collecting money on Wednesday nights to greeting visitors at funerals to stuffing notebooks for Bible studies, these are the women you want to call if your tasks have overwhelmed you and you need willing and competent hands to make short work of any large task.

I think of the many with the gift of administration like Jo and Rhonda. I see Anna who has served as a lovely model of Christian womanhood for young women from middle school through college. I think of Jan who with zest and creativity serves the needs of women who are often forgotten, the older single women. I think of Rachel who serves in many ways, but who sacrificially scoops that cold ice cream at Wednesday night dinners and does so with the most beautiful smile I have ever seen. I think of Karen who writes cards to widows on their birthdays. Pat Holder comes to mind who uses her artistry to create exquisite handmade cards for many events and serves in countless other ways. I think of our pastor's wife, so humble in her role that requires difficult travel, much prayer, and denying herself the luxury of having control of her schedule. I think of all the women who faithfully pray in all the many prayer groups around our church, a very hidden ministry.

The Body of Christ is not complete without these women. When I think of the church, I do not think of the beautiful edifice that is our church- I think of these women. They allow the Lord to use them with no expectation of a thank you or recognition, and I can see the joy in their faces that results from their submission to anything He wants, no matter how humble.

These are women who are trying to pattern their lives after Jesus:

3 Do nothing from selfish ambition or conceit, but in humility count others more significant than yourselves. 4 Let each of you look not only to his own interests, but also to the interests of others. 5 Have this mind among yourselves, which is yours in Christ Jesus, 6 who, though he was in the form of God, did not count equality with God a thing to be grasped, 7 but emptied himself, by taking the form of a servant, being born in the likeness of men. Philippians 2:3-7

These are women who understand all Paul was saying when he taught about using whatever gifts we are given for Him and for His church. They will not be the women who will be at the front of the room as a teacher or leader; they will be in the back of the room making name badges and helping a visitor find her way. These are women who are good stewards of whatever gift God has given them as Peter exhorted us to do:

10 As each has received a gift, use it to serve one another, as good stewards of God's varied grace… I Peter 4:10a

These are women who live out what Paul said in Romans 12:6a to all Christ-followers:

6 *Having gifts that differ according to the grace given to us, let us use them…*

I hope I get to stand near these women in Heaven just to be near enough to see what happens when God greets them and they reminisce together about all they humbly did for Him. These are the ones who made themselves servants so that He could be elevated in the eyes of others. Oh, what glory is ahead for them!

DEVOTIONAL 22: MEMORIAL DAY: WHY CHRISTIANS HONOR VETERANS AND FALLEN SOLDIERS

Jesus was a revolutionary. He changed the world, yet He was respectful to authorities (Romans 13:1-7) and supported the laws of His country, such as paying taxes (Matthew 17: 24-27.) He was bold and courageous when it was needed but knew when to be silent and stand mute if that were wiser. He paid a staggering price for our freedom from sin, leaving Heaven and suffering separation from His Father so that we could be free from sin and live with Him for eternity in Heaven. He died for us when we were yet His enemies.

On a mortal level, the soldiers who have freely given their lives to ensure our freedom have died, in part, so we can openly worship Jesus Christ. Religious freedom is one of our most precious freedoms and has been constantly threatened since persecuted Christians first landed here, seeking a safe place to worship. These freedoms are being threatened today more aggressively than ever before, and the attacks are from within and from without.

Christians are the most patriotic people group in the United States. Some will challenge that statement, but when I listen to the rhetoric from other groups, I do not hear the call to patriotism that I hear from Christians. I do not hear the expressions of love for our country, the support for her, the pride in her, nor the commitment to her. Although Christians should not be blind to righting policies that need to be righted nor unwilling to admit our country's mistakes, we tend to look at those needs as isolated issues to be addressed rather than a reason to make blanket, derogatory statements about the United States of America. No matter what your party, supporting the United States in the global neighborhood should be an understood responsibility of every citizen. Why is this a topic in a Christian blog?

Because on days like Memorial Day, we need to remember why Christians, in particular, should be overwhelmed with gratitude for the price our veterans and fallen soldiers have paid for our freedom to worship. Psalm 33:12 says, *"Blessed is the nation whose God is the Lord, the people whom he has chosen as his heritage!"*

Although Memorial Day honors those who paid the ultimate price to protect you and me, I always take this chance to thank our veterans who had a moment when they made up their minds that they were WILLING to pay that ultimate price as well. Here are just a few of the many reasons we should say a prayer this week for a person who lost a family member in the military or who has someone currently in grave danger in the service:

1. The freedom to practice our religion according to our beliefs was paid for in the Revolutionary War.

2. The World Wars, Korean War, Vietnam War and wars in Afghanistan, Iraq, and many other locales have preserved our land from the ever-encroaching enemies of the United States. In almost every case, those who would attack and conquer us do not believe in Jehovah God. Many of these religions have stated purposes to destroy anyone who will not convert to their religion. One example of that can be read about in Michael Youssef's excellent book, **The Third Jihad**. Who knows what religion would be the predominant one in the United States today if men and women had not knowingly laid down their lives for our right to worship Jehovah? Although these other religions are encroaching on our freedoms and influencing many not to believe in our God, the men and women who have died have effectively kept us a Christian nation for over 200 years.

Even as we speak, men and women are fighting or preparing to fight our battles for our freedom all over the world, and especially in the Middle East. They operate dangerous equipment, live in dire weather conditions, face physical and mental opposition daily, and wake up every morning making the choice to die if necessary that day.

Please take a moment to read the verses at the end of this blog, and then consider doing one of the following to honor those who fought for you to be able to casually walk into a church, worship openly, own a Bible you don't have to hide, and say that you believe in Jesus Christ as your Savior and the one and only way to the Father and eternal life. Millions of people right now around the world ache for those freedoms and are deprived. Below are some things you can do to acknowledge that these privileges did not come easily and were paid for with the blood of people who were loved and counted on and are still missed:

1. Talk to some of your friends in their eighties, and ask them if they knew anyone who was lost in a war. I have a dear friend whose charming, gifted, lively brother died when he was shot down in World War II. She still thinks about him. Acknowledging the people who suffered the loss of loved ones is one way to honor the fallen heroes.

2. Consider how you can support a woman who is single-parenting while her husband is deployed. Money is probably tight for babysitting or a nice dinner she does not have to cook, and you could supply both. She may just need someone to listen. She may need Jesus, a good church, or someone to tell her she is doing a good job.

3. Contact the many organizations that support living veterans: Wounded Warriors, USO, Student Veterans of America, the Elizabeth Dole foundation, etc.

4. Pray for those currently on active duty. Find out who in your church has a son or daughter in active service, especially those that are far from home. Let their families know you are supporting their child and them in prayer until he or she is safely home. Consider writing a letter to the service person; let him or her know you care and are praying.

5. Look for clues someone is a veteran, like the wonderful young man who repaired my stovetop this week. A remark made me think he might have learned his skills in the military, so I asked him and then thanked him. He has had a difficult time since returning, and I talked to him a bit about the Lord.

6. Thank God for anyone you know who was or is a veteran. I thank God for my Dad who was a much decorated war hero but kept it a secret until my uncle spilled his secret shortly before Dad's death. Most real heroes are like this, never acknowledging the price they paid for your freedom and mine.

Verses to Consider this Memorial Day

A pop culture trend is to believe that Christians should never take up weapons, but that is not what the Bible says. Yes, Jesus came to bring us peace, but it is a peace the world does not understand. How could the following verses encourage a soldier, give you insight into Jesus, the real peacekeeper, or otherwise be food for thought this Memorial Day?

JOHN 15:13

Greater love hath no man than this, that a man lay down his life for his friends. KJV

ROMANS 13:1-5

Let every person be subject to the governing authorities. For there is no authority except from God, and those that exist have been instituted by God. Therefore whoever resists the authorities resists what God has appointed, and those who resist will incur judgment. For rulers are not a terror to good conduct, but to bad. Would you have no fear of the one who is in authority? Then do what is good, and you will receive his approval, for he is God's servant for your good. But if you do wrong, be afraid, for he does not bear the sword in vain. For he is the servant of God, an avenger who carries out God's wrath on the wrongdoer. Therefore one must be in subjection, not only to avoid God's wrath but also for the sake of conscience.

1 TIMOTHY 2:1-6

First of all, then, I urge that supplications, prayers, intercessions, and thanksgivings be made for all people, for kings and all who are in high positions, that we may lead a peaceful and quiet life, godly and dignified in every way. This is good, and it is pleasing in the sight of God our Savior, who desires all people to be saved and to come to the knowledge of the truth. For there is one God, and there is one mediator between God and men, the man Christ Jesus, ...

GENESIS 14:14-15

When Abram heard that his kinsman had been taken captive, he led forth his trained men, born in his house, 318 of them, and went in pursuit as far as Dan. And he divided his forces against them by night, he and his servants, and defeated them and pursued them to Hobah, north of Damascus.

MATTHEW 24:6-8

And you will hear of wars and rumors of wars. See that you are not alarmed, for this must take place, but the end is not yet. For nation will rise against nation, and kingdom against kingdom, and there will be famines and earthquakes in various places. All these are but the beginning of the birth pains.

PSALM 91:1-16

He who dwells in the shelter of the Most High will abide in the shadow of the Almighty. I will say to the Lord, "My refuge and my fortress, my God, in whom I trust." For he will deliver you from the snare of the fowler and from the deadly pestilence. He will cover you with his pinions, and under his wings you will find refuge; his faithfulness is a shield and buckler. You will not fear the terror of the night, nor the arrow that flies by day, .

PSALM 108:12-13

Oh grant us help against the foe, for vain is the salvation of man! With God we shall do valiantly; it is he who will tread down our foes.

MATTHEW 23:11

The greatest among you shall be your servant.

1 SAMUEL 30:8

And David inquired of the Lord, "Shall I pursue after this band? Shall I overtake them?" He answered him, "Pursue, for you shall surely overtake and shall surely rescue."

ROMANS 12:9-13

Let love be genuine. Abhor what is evil; hold fast to what is good. Love one another with brotherly affection. Outdo one another in showing honor. Do not be slothful in zeal, be fervent in spirit, serve the Lord. Rejoice in hope, be patient in tribulation, be constant in prayer. Contribute to the needs of the saints and seek to show hospitality.

MATTHEW 27:54

When the centurion and those who were with him, keeping watch over Jesus, saw the earthquake and what took place, they were filled with awe and said, "Truly this was the Son of God!"

PSALM 34:18

The Lord is near to the brokenhearted and saves the crushed in spirit.

DEVOTIONAL 23: MARY OF BETHANY: A MODEL OF ACCEPTING JESUS' LOVE AND STRENGTH

One of the most convicting stories in the Bible for me personally is the story of Mary and Martha. These two women, along with their brother Lazarus, were some of Jesus' dearest friends. Over the next couple of weeks, we will look at the very different relationship Jesus had with each sister, as unique as they were. Before we look at their story, I would like to address some controversies about who Mary is. My take on her identity is that it does not matter to me whether Mary Magdalene and Mary of Bethany are the same person. Most modern Western scholars say they are separate individuals, mainly based on the hometowns attached to their names, but some Medieval scholars said they were the same woman. Some scholars believe Luke kept the identity of Mary Magdalene a secret in His telling of parts of the story because of the reference to her sinful past. I am with Luke in letting that part of Mary's past remain anonymous. *"All have sinned and come short of the glory of God,"* (Romans 3:23), so particulars like this are unimportant to me. I also have a strong conviction from the Lord from I Timothy 1:4, *"**4** nor to devote themselves to myths and endless genealogies, which promote speculations rather than the stewardship from God that is by faith."* I just don't believe God wants us to spend inordinate time speculating over these things and especially not arguing among ourselves about them. Whatever her past, Mary at the time of these stories is clearly covered with the righteousness of Jesus, a true saint.

The story that comforts me most about Mary takes place when her brother Lazarus dies. The story does not say Jesus wept when He heard Lazarus had died. Jesus wept over the loss of His friend **only after** he encountered the griefstricken sisters. In particular, sister Mary was in need of consolation and comfort. How do we know this? She has not come to meet Jesus as her sister Martha did. Mary stays in her house, being consoled by neighbors according to John 11:31, and does not come at first to greet Jesus as He nears her home. Then verse 33 says, *"When Jesus saw her weeping, and the Jews who had come with her also weeping, he was deeply moved in his spirit* *and greatly troubled."* Two verses later, John 35 says simply, "Jesus wept."

In other words, Jesus cried with her. If you have ever had a friend so moved by your grief she cries when you cry, you understand the love of a friend who is moved by your tears. Jesus is moved by our tears, our loneliness, our hurts. He is moved right now by whatever you are suffering.

Mary did not have to act strong. She did not have to quote passages of memorized Scripture. She just needed to come to Jesus and let Him see her pain. That is all He wants from us all—that we would come to Him in honesty and humility and show Him our true self. Mary seems to have the unusual ability to be honest about her weakness and inability to help herself. Maybe that is why Jesus was able to work one of the most profound recorded miracles in her life. She came to Him in helplessness and with no strength or ability of her own to fix her circumstances. He did not need to strip her of that before He could be sovereign over her situation.

What situation in your life do you need to bring to Jesus and confess your helplessness and need of Him? Do not guide or direct Him with your opinions. Express your dependence on Him and hand over the death of a dream or a situation to Him. Ask Him to do what He thinks best, in His timing. When you do, be prepared that His timing may look as bleak in the short term as the death of Lazarus looked to Mary and Martha. Choose to trust Him anyway. He will come to you in His way. He will love you and grieve with you and comfort you. He loves you as He loved Mary, and you need to do nothing to merit it. Just accept it, and allow Him to love you and to handle your grief or loss His way.

The Story of Lazarus (ESV) is printed below for your convenience in case you have not read it recently.

11 Now a certain man was ill, Lazarus of Bethany, the village of Mary and her sister Martha. 2 It was Mary who anointed the Lord with ointment and wiped his feet with her hair, whose brother Lazarus was ill.3 So the sisters sent to him, saying, "Lord, he whom you love is ill." 4 But when Jesus heard it he said, "This illness does not lead to death. It is for the glory of God, so that the Son of God may be glorified through it."

5 Now Jesus loved Martha and her sister and Lazarus. 6 So, when he heard that Lazarus[a] was ill, he stayed two days longer in the place where he was. 7 Then after this he said to the disciples, "Let us go to Judea again." 8 The disciples said to him, "Rabbi, the Jews were just now seeking to stone you, and are you going there again?" 9 Jesus answered, "Are there not twelve hours in the day? If anyone walks in the day, he does not stumble, because he sees the light of this world. 10 But if anyone walks in the night, he stumbles, because the light is not in him."11 After saying these things, he said to them, "Our friend Lazarus has fallen asleep, but I go to awaken him." 12 The disciples said to him, "Lord, if he has fallen asleep, he will recover." 13 Now Jesus had spoken of his death, but they thought that he meant taking rest in sleep.14 Then Jesus told them plainly, "Lazarus has died, 15 and for your sake I am glad that I was not there, so that you may believe. But let us go to him." 16 So Thomas, called the Twin,[b] said to his fellow disciples, "Let us also go, that we may die with him."

I AM THE RESURRECTION AND THE LIFE

17 Now when Jesus came, he found that Lazarus had already been in the tomb four days. 18 Bethany was near Jerusalem, about two miles[c] off,19 and many of the Jews had come to Martha and Mary to console them concerning their brother. 20 So when Martha heard that Jesus was coming, she went and met him, but Mary remained seated in the house.21 Martha said to Jesus, "Lord, if you had been here, my brother would not have died. 22 But even now I know that whatever you ask from God, God will give you." 23 Jesus said to her, "Your brother will rise again."24 Martha said to him, "I know that he will rise again in the resurrection on the last day." 25 Jesus said to her, "I am the resurrection and the life.[d] Whoever believes in me, though he die, yet shall he live, **26** and everyone who lives and believes in me shall never die. Do you believe this?" **27** She said to him, "Yes, Lord; I believe that you are the Christ, the Son of God, who is coming into the world."

JESUS WEEPS

28 When she had said this, she went and called her sister Mary, saying in private, "The Teacher is here and is calling for you." **29** And when she heard it, she rose quickly and went to him. **30** Now Jesus had not yet come into the village, but was still in the place where Martha had met him. **31** When the Jews who were with her in the house, consoling her, saw Mary rise quickly and go out, they followed her, supposing that she was going to the tomb to weep there. **32** Now when Mary came to where Jesus was and saw him, she fell at his feet, saying to him, "Lord, if you had been here, my brother would not have died." **33** When Jesus saw her weeping, and the Jews who had come with her also weeping, he was deeply moved[e] in his spirit and greatly troubled. **34** And he said, "Where have you laid him?" They said to him, "Lord, come and see." **35** Jesus wept. **36** So the Jews said, "See how he loved him!" **37** But some of them said, "Could not he who opened the eyes of the blind man also have kept this man from dying?

JESUS RAISES LAZARUS
38 Then Jesus, deeply moved again, came to the tomb. It was a cave, and a stone lay against it. **39** Jesus said, "Take away the stone." Martha, the sister of the dead man, said to him, "Lord, by this time there will be an odor, for he has been dead four days." **40** Jesus said to her, "Did I not tell you that if you believed you would see the glory of God?" **41** So they took away the stone. And Jesus lifted up his eyes and said, "Father, I thank you that you have heard me. **42** I knew that you always hear me, but I said this on account of the people standing around, that they may believe that you sent me." **43** When he had said these things, he cried out with a loud voice, "Lazarus, come out." **44** The man who had died came out, his hands and feet bound with linen strips, and his face wrapped with a cloth. Jesus said to them, "Unbind him, and let him go."

DEVOTIONAL 24: THE HEART CRY OF GOD

A Father's Day Message

To me, some of the most poignant words in all the Bible are David's cry of grief upon hearing the news of his son's death. This son who had betrayed him, tried to steal his throne, and brought so much pain to the family for years was the object of so much love and grief and loss that you can hear it in his father's gut-wrenching cries:

"O my son Absalom, my son, my son Absalom! Would I had died instead of you, O Absalom, my son, my son!" 2 Samuel 18:33b

Can you hear this father crying out from the deepest part of his soul? Sonship is very important to the Lord, and we daughters share in the Father's love equally. Every word in the Bible is the inspired Word of God, and He carefully placed this story for us to read and consider. God is intentional about portraying the depth of a Father's love because He wants us to know the depth of **His** love and compassion for us. Stories such as the prodigal son reach out from the pages of our Bibles and cause us to marvel at the wide and deep love that only a parent can know for a child. And just as important, each of these stories portrays forgiveness and grace so wide and deep that nothing else on earth can compare to it. Such is the heart cry of the Lord for His children, you and me.

The Bible calls David "a man after God's own heart." Through David, God chooses to show us how a Father loves despite the worst treachery and rebellion on a child's part. It shows love beyond reason or worldly standards. When God chose that story to be shared, I believe he was saying, "This is what a Father does. This is the mercy and unmovable love I have for you." God allows us to see this love of a father when the ungrateful, insulting prodigal son in Luke 15 finally returns home because he has nowhere else to turn. As he approaches his father's home, we see the Father running to embrace him and welcome him and bless him. My pastor says that running is a major indignity for a Middle Eastern man. This full out running toward his son is such a passionate expression of love and acceptance that we understand what "all is forgiven" really means.

God wants us to know how much He loves us. He loves us more than David loved Absalom, more than the prodigal's father loved him, and even more than your parents loved you or that you love your children. And His is a perfect love. His love is consistent and never falters or makes mistakes. He loves us no matter what we have done in our past and no matter how we have worked against Him or spoken ill of Him. Through the stories He inspired of fathers who have hearts like His, He is speaking His love to us.

Many of the Biblical stories that illustrate God's love for us are told as a father's love for the nation of Israel. When we see God's love for Israel in Isaiah 62:5, we get some insight into how God loves.

Behold, the Lord has proclaimed
   to the end of the earth:
Say to the daughter of Zion,
   "Behold, your salvation comes;
behold, his reward is with him,
   and his recompense before him."
12 *And they shall be called The Holy People,*
   The Redeemed of the Lord;
and you shall be called Sought Out,
   A City Not Forsaken.

Just like Jerusalem (Zion), we have been "sought out." In our case, we were sought by Jesus Christ who came expressly for us and who paid the price for all of our sin. *He will never leave us or forsake us* (Hebrews 13:5).

Yet like the Israelites, we have a choice to turn away from our Father and reject this rich and overflowing love. When the Pharisees were publicly rejecting Him and intent on doing Him harm, this is how Jesus responds to them:

"Jerusalem, Jerusalem, you who kill the prophets and stone those sent to you, how often I have longed to gather your children together, as a hen gathers her chicks under her wings, and you were not willing."

This is the heart cry of a parent. This is the love that lives in the depths of a parent's heart no matter the age of a child or whatever the child's choices in life have been. That longing to gather your child to you is just that—longing. It is up to the child to accept the love and protection and blessing of a parent, but not all are willing. In this case, Jerusalem was not willing, and shortly thereafter they crucified Jesus.

Yet, He loves us still. He still longs to gather each person to Himself and show His love to us. What about you? Are you willing? God is calling out to you through His Word, through this blog, through ways you may not have stopped to acknowledge. Will you turn toward Him? He will come running to embrace you and support you for the rest of your life.

(Next week, we will continue to think about God's feelings for us and what His tender love looks like. The story of the prodigal son is below.)

Luke 15:11-32

11 And he said, "There was a man who had two sons. 12 And the younger of them said to his father, 'Father, give me the share of property that is coming to me.' And he divided his property between them. 13 Not many days later, the younger son gathered all he had and took a journey into a far country, and there he squandered his property in reckless living.14 And when he had spent everything, a severe famine arose in that country, and he began to be in need. 15 So he went and hired himself out to[b] one of the citizens of that country, who sent him into his fields to feed pigs. 16 And he was longing to be fed with the pods that the pigs ate, and no one gave him anything.

17 *"But when he came to himself, he said, 'How many of my father's hired servants have more than enough bread, but I perish here with hunger!* *18* *I will arise and go to my father, and I will say to him, "Father, I have sinned against heaven and before you.* *19* *I am no longer worthy to be called your son. Treat me as one of your hired servants."'* *20* *And he arose and came to his father. But while he was still a long way off, his father saw him and felt compassion, and ran and embraced him and kissed him.* *21* *And the son said to him, 'Father, I have sinned against heaven and before you. I am no longer worthy to be called your son.'[c]* *22* *But the father said to his servants,[d] 'Bring quickly the best robe, and put it on him, and put a ring on his hand, and shoes on his feet.* *23* *And bring the fattened calf and kill it, and let us eat and celebrate.* *24* *For this my son was dead, and is alive again; he was lost, and is found.' And they began to celebrate.*

25 *"Now his older son was in the field, and as he came and drew near to the house, he heard music and dancing.* *26* *And he called one of the servants and asked what these things meant.* *27* *And he said to him, 'Your brother has come, and your father has killed the fattened calf, because he has received him back safe and sound.'* *28* *But he was angry and refused to go in. His father came out and entreated him,* *29* *but he answered his father, 'Look, these many years I have served you, and I never disobeyed your command, yet you never gave me a young goat, that I might celebrate with my friends.* *30* *But when this son of yours came, who has devoured your property with prostitutes, you killed the fattened calf for him!'* *31* *And he said to him, 'Son, you are always with me, and all that is mine is yours.* *32* *It was fitting to celebrate and be glad, for this your brother was dead, and is alive; he was lost, and is found.'"*

DEVOTIONAL 25: HOW DOES GOD FEEL ABOUT YOU?

John 11:35 is the shortest verse of the Bible but one of the most profound for those of us who want to know Him more deeply and intimately. It says simply, "Jesus wept."

We gain deep and revealing insight into the heart of Jesus from this passage. Because He knows what it is to shed tears from a broken heart, He understands our tears.

And your tears are noted individually. Jesus keeps account of them and does not forget or lose track of your suffering through the years. Hundreds of years before this touching scene, a psalmist wrote:

8 You have kept count of my tossings;
put my tears in your bottle.
Are they not in your book? (Psalm 56:8)

Did you know that your tears are that precious to Him? That He feels your losses and your pain? Jesus came to earth and experienced human pain so He could not just sympathize but empathize. Most scholars believe Jesus lost His father at a young age. He knew grief. In fact, Isaiah 53:3-4 foretells the coming of Jesus and describes Him this way:

"He was despised and rejected by men, a man of sorrows and acquainted with grief; and as one from whom men hide their faces he was despised, and we esteemed him not. Surely he has borne our griefs and carried our sorrows; yet we esteemed him stricken, smitten by God, and afflicted."

You have never had a friend or family member who so deeply feels your pain and understands firsthand any sense of loss you may be experiencing.

But not all of your life is about loss and pain, and not all of the Lord's feelings about you are sympathy and consolation. He also feels joy beyond description at the thought of you. It is literally inexpressible as I am told that the English language does not have adequate words to translate how God feels about you. The second half of Zephaniah 3:17 says it best:

… he will rejoice over you with gladness;
*   he will quiet you by his love;*
he will exult over you with loud singing.

The words *"rejoice over you with gladness"* is the phrase that has no exact translation into English. The NASB says *"exult over you."* The NIV says *"take great delight in you."* I am told that the actual Hebrew words express an outburst of such joy and exultation that it is more like a dance and a song, even a leap of joy. God is so delighted at the thought of you that He dances over you with joy and singing. This is the same God who knows every sin you have ever committed, and He loves you this much anyway. This is amazing love that the world can't give nor take away, no matter what happens.

Please take just a moment to sit with God to let Him rejoice over you. Then express your feelings to Him. He loves hearing from His children about their feelings, especially their feelings toward Him. And be honest. You may be suffering from some feelings that are not delightful. He wants to hear it all from your heart to His. He will still delight in you, and if there are tears, He will be moved by them and comfort you. Just talk to Him. Form or format are not important to Him. Eyes opened or closed, have a conversation with God and see what happens in the days to come.

DEVOTIONAL 26: MARTHA: LEARNING THAT HIS LOVE IS ENOUGH

NOTE: This week, after a 2-week focus on fathers, we will return to the story of Martha and Mary.

Though I aspire to be like Mary, my nature tends to be more like Martha's. I remember my chagrin when I first saw myself in Martha, especially in the telling of the story of Lazarus' death in *Luke 10:38-42*:

38 Now as they went on their way, Jesus entered a village. And a woman named Martha welcomed him into her house. 39 And she had a sister called Mary, who sat at the Lord's feet and listened to his teaching.40 But Martha was distracted with much serving. And she went up to him and said, "Lord, do you not care that my sister has left me to serve alone? Tell her then to help me." 41 But the Lord answered her, "Martha, Martha, you are anxious and troubled about many things, 42 but one thing is necessary. Mary has chosen the good portion, which will not be taken away from her."

When I realized that Mary had *"chosen what is better (NIV),"* it really bothered me because my earthly impetus is to take things into my own hands and act and do. As an oldest child, I was encouraged to be self-reliant, to see needs and act on them, to pitch in. All of this was good training, and I am grateful to my parents for it, but every good thing God and our parents give us can be taken one step too far. When we go even an inch beyond what God has planned for us, a good thing can become something harmful to our relationship with Him—even service.

Martha's barrier to all the love the Lord wanted to give her was not her service. Her service was a good thing. But she allowed her service to be her focal point instead of the person of Jesus. As she served, she was preparing for Jesus to come visit her home. But when He arrived, she did not break from her preparations just to be with Him. Her focus was still on what she was *doing* for Him and rather than having her eyes on *HIM*. She did not value simply being in His presence as much as she valued her own preparations. She loved her act of service and was probably a little proud to present it to Him. But all He really wanted was for her to sit down with Him and let Him look into her face and tell her He loved her. She was distracted from this communion and fellowship by her serving. Her serving actually got in the way of her receiving love and communication from Him.

Has this ever happened to you? Have you ever been so focused on making your act of service so excellent that you neglected just the unhurried time you needed in Jesus' company? Is it hard for you to just enjoy His company in the midst of your preparations and service? I confess I have to stay in prayer on this.

Another distraction for Martha was that her eyes were on Mary more than on Jesus. As she watched Mary not helping with the preparations, Martha shifted her focus away from the joy of the time with Jesus and placed it on her sister. If Martha had only kept her eyes and thoughts on Jesus, she could not have dwelt on Mary's shortcomings. She may have glanced at them (we are not blind to events), but this annoyance would have been secondary to the joy of being with Jesus. She could have kept her mind stayed on Him instead of on Mary. This annoyance could not have grown to the point that she spent her valuable time with the Lord discussing the petty details of housekeeping and sibling conflict instead of exchanging expressions of love.

What if the Lord said to you, "I plan to come to your house next week from 9:00-10:00AM, and you can ask me anything, express to me how you feel about me, and generally use the time any way you choose." That hour would be precious. Would you use it to talk to Him about something as trivial as housekeeping details and disappointment in a sibling? That is what Martha did.

And we often do just that as Jesus shows up daily for us in our prayer time and in our daily walk with Him. Yes, we should tell Him everything, but look at the balance of your time with Him. Is the majority spent in love and worship or is the majority spent on the details of life? What are you doing with your precious conversation time with the Lord?

Jesus loved Martha. He mentions her by name and He walks with her. He just wants more of her time. He just wants her to relax and rest in His presence. And that is what He wants from us.

DEVOTIONAL 27: MARY MAGDALENE: HEALED TO LOVE AND SERVE

I realized recently how often I refer to one of the many women that Christ counted among his friends and followers, Mary Magdalene. On Easter, I wrote:

"Jesus appeared to Mary Magdalene just after He had risen. She was going about a normal Sunday morning (Mark 16:2) when she turned and there was Jesus (verse 9)! She is so stunned that she cannot comprehend this is Jesus, but then He speaks her name and she knows (John 20:16)."

Mark 16:9 tells us that after the ordeal of grief that was the crucifixion and burial, He chose to appear first to this Mary, before anyone else. What an honor. It reveals the beautiful and pure intimacy of their relationship, a relationship of appreciation and regard, not a conventional male-female relationship. She knows His voice, and she knows when He is calling her name.

But just because she was chosen to be the first one to see the Resurrected Jesus and to be His messenger to go back and tell the disciples about it did not mean they would honor her or even believe her. Luke 24:11 gives their response to her news:

"11 but these words seemed to them an idle tale, and they did not believe them."

Just because Jesus has singled us out to be His child and even given us a mission and assignment in life does not mean the world will recognize it or give us any favor. We may feel like a failure when we try to deliver the Good News that Christ has arisen, and we may be disrespected by Christians and nonChristians alike when we try to live out the task He has given us to do. Because He gives each of His children a unique path to walk, He often tells them to do very different things. Sometimes, He has one daughter live a very public life, teaching or gaining accolades in any number of ways. He may have another daughter like Wanzie at our church who quietly prays over prayer requests in solitude, who has little or no public recognition, even after years of devoted service in the solitude of her prayer room. We each have to walk the path He gave us that leads us on our journey home to Him.

We may also be disrespected because of our past. Certainly, there were people who knew Mary Magdalene before she met Jesus who may have doubted she could ever be considered a righteous woman. Shortly after Jesus began His ministry and began doing miraculous healings, He healed Mary Magdalene of either a physical or mental disorder. Luke 8:1-3 says:

"8 Soon afterward he went on through cities and villages, proclaiming and bringing the good news of the kingdom of God. And the twelve were with him, 2 and also some women who had been healed of evil spirits and infirmities: Mary, called Magdalene, from whom seven demons had gone out, 3 and Joanna, the wife of Chuza, Herod's household manager, and Susanna, and many others, who provided for them out of their means."

When we come to Jesus and are changed, it often takes a long time for those around us to believe that the change is genuine. I know that many of my friends thought I was a hypocrite because one day I shared their worldly values and then overnight I was a different person, seeing the world more through the eyes of Christ than through any other lens. I did not blame them. I was not the same person and the change was abrupt. Even one of my sisters who was very much of the mind that all Christians were judgmental hypocrites doubted the transformation. She finally came to me with her questions about the Lord because she said, "I know you really know Him." It took many years,

Knowing Him is an honor. Mary Magdalene was honored to be selected to see Him. I have moments of incredulity every day that He has allowed me to know Him and know Him well. Like Mary Magdalene, there is an intimacy in our relationship, and He reveals things about Himself to me all the time, usually when I am alone reading His Word in the mornings. He gives me that glimpse of some truth about him and I just say, "Thank you, Lord."

So what is the response to this honor? Like Mary Magdalene did, it is to go and tell others that He lives and that you have seen Him, maybe with the eyes of your heart, but you have seen that He is alive and real. He is not the historic Jesus to you; He is your intimate friend.

And verse 3 above says that Mary was one of the women who served the apostles in their missionary work and *"who provided for them out of their means."* Like Mary, the response to being honored by having Jesus reveal Himself to us is to use whatever gifts we have been given to go and tell the Good News or support those who do.

Mary is such a Christlike example of another thing we should do in response to being allowed to see Jesus. She not only ministers to the apostles but to the Body of Christ. We see her serving in every humble and lowly way, doing jobs that are not always pleasant. She accompanies Mary, the mother of Jesus, as they stand at a distance and watch her son die an excruciating death. Quite often, serving the Body means just being there. John 19:25 says:

Near the cross of Jesus stood his mother, his mother's sister, Mary the wife of Clopas, and Mary Magdalene.

Later, it was Mary and two other women who came to anoint the body of Jesus with spices for burial.

Mary was there for Jesus to minister to the financial needs of His ministry, to minister to His body in death, and to minister to His people as she ran back to tell them the Good News. Her life pretty much says it all: No matter what our past life has been, once Jesus shows Himself to you, you are covered with His perfect righteousness and are part of His family. What will you do in response to that?

(Note: There are some controversial *man-made* theories about Mary Magdalene that will not be addressed in this blog because they are false. Only Biblical, factual events will be included in this content.)

DEVOTIONAL 28: UNDER ATTACK

Yesterday, I became acutely aware that I am under attack. Sometimes satan tips his hand and shows himself. We clearly see what he is up to.

Have you ever felt under attack? If you are following hard after the Lord, you have surely experienced an assault on your health or relationships or finances or peace or all of the above at once. Satan will often leave untouched those who are following him, but will harass those earnestly seeking to follow Jesus. He cannot defeat us, but he has ploys to discourage us and to distract us from fixing our gaze on the Lord.

These attacks may take the form of things in our lives going inexplicably wrong. Or, in my case recently, we may have an onslaught of negative emotions like guilt, regret, frustration, disappointment, or sadness. What are we to do when these attacks occur?

1. **First, recognize the enemy's tactics.**

When yesterday I was flooded with annoyance over the behavior of another, I could feel my flesh rising up—and not in a good way. I tried to toss it to the Lord (*"casting all (my) anxieties on him, because he cares for (me)."* I Peter 5:7), but I did not really stop and engage earnestly with the Lord. It was more like a quick arrow prayer shot up to Heaven as I proceeded with my schedule as planned. That was my first mistake. If a mugger had jumped out at me in a parking lot, I would not have shrugged it off. Satan was trying to spiritually mug me, and I barely paused to ask God's help.

By dinner, I was feeling spiritually out of sorts. Now you have to understand that I am not prone to emotional lows or depression. Almost all the wonderful Christians in my family struggle with this chemical reality, but that is not the usual for me. The only time I ever thought I might be depressed, I went to the doctor for a physical. Turned out that the loss of appetite and energy was not depression- I was pregnant! So since I knew this was not the case this time (:), I was now aware that I was emotionally a bit low. When my son spontaneously called and said, "Let's go to dinner," I jumped at the chance to escape and enjoy the company of one I know who loves me. I should have first spent some time with THE ONE I know who loves me.

During the conversation, I made a prideful remark about something that happened 35 years ago. I don't think my son even realized it, but I was ashamed of not being a better example for him. After I returned home, the enemy badgered me about that prideful remark until I finally fell asleep after much tossing and turning. I should have stopped then and spent quality time with the Lord, but I was tired, another tactic the enemy uses to keep me from pressing in hard with the Lord. I did pray a bit, but mostly for the requests of others when my own soul was badly in need of prayer. If I had recognized the full-blown battle I was in and run full speed into the arms of Jesus, I would have had a more restful night and would not have carried that yuckiness into this new, beautiful day.

2. Second, don't procrastinate about repentance.

So the enemy uses guilt and regret liberally to replace thoughts of the Lord with thoughts of my own missteps. I forget to take that first step to stop everything and spend time in true repentance. Instead, I tell myself I will address it later, maybe tomorrow in my quiet time. I delay. I forget that if I will repent and ask God to take my sin that He will *"remember my sins no more," Hebrews 8:12.* In the moment, I forget that *"there is therefore now no condemnation for those who are in Christ Jesus," Romans 8:1.* I forget that addressing my sin sooner rather than later brings blessed relief. Every time I go through this process of authentic repentance, I think, "Why did I put this off? I feel so much better!"

In the process of repenting of the sins I knew about, God revealed some other sins I had not slowed down enough to notice previously. All the yucky emotions that brought me to this point served to give God an open door to my heart. He was able to do the good, deep cleaning my heart badly needed. I will be a better friend and a better family member because of the last 24 hours of yuckiness.

3. Get your focus off yourself

Self-focus is one of the enemy's favorite ploys to dilute my energy and worship. Our God is a *"do unto others as you would have them do unto you"* God. He is a *"Let no one seek his own good, but that of his neighbor"* kind of God *(I Corinthians 10:24.)* He is a God who says we should be washing our brothers' dirty feet and not waiting for someone to come wash ours, *(John 13:12-15.)* Think about the Lord and His attributes. Think about the people He has placed in your life to serve. In other words, think of others and not yourself, not even your sin, once you have truly repented.

4. Finally, move on

When I indulge in going over and over what is bothering me about me without turning it over to the Lord, it is a type of self-absorption He did not intend for me. Yes, He wants me to acknowledge and repent of my sin, but then He wants me to let Him take it from me. He wants me to move on. My flesh tends to want to hold on to it, to let it be a part of my identity and my story. It is not. He wants it to be *"as far as the east is from the west,"* but He cannot remove it that far if I keep recalling it.

as far as the east is from the west,
   so far does he remove our transgressions from us. Psalm 103:12.

I think Paul, a notorious transformed sinner, says it best in Philippians 3:12-15:

"12 Not that I have already obtained this or am already perfect, but I press on to make it my own, because Christ Jesus has made me his own. 13 Brothers, I do not consider that I have made it my own. But one thing I do: forgetting what lies behind and straining forward to what lies ahead, 14 I press on toward the goal for the prize of the upward call of God in Christ Jesus. 15 Let those of us who are mature think this way, and if in anything you think otherwise, God will reveal that also to you."

If anyone had grounds to recall his sin, it was Paul. John Piper at desiringGod.com says that in Philippians 3, Paul is saying, "I am not paralyzed by the horrible memories of the fact that I was killing Christians. I was throwing them in prison. I was shaking my fist in the face of God ... I am forgetting all of that and I am pressing on."

Paul fully accepted God's forgiveness of his great body of sin and did not let the past keep dragging him backward. Instead, Paul had perhaps one of the most world-changing effective ministries of all time, second only to Jesus Himself. That's what really accepting that you are forgiven can do. It frees you to live today for Him because yesterday is not your captor. Do you need to pray for your own submission to fully accept all the Grace He wants to give you today?

NOTE: Some Christians do not believe in discussing being under attack because it gives our enemy too much credit. I believe in acknowledging the enemy while at the same time rejoicing that *"he who is in you is greater than he who is in the world," (I John 4:4.)* The battle is ultimately already won, but we are still on the front lines.

More power verses from Paul:

But he said to me, "My grace is sufficient for you, for my power is made perfect in weakness." Therefore I will boast all the more gladly of my weaknesses, so that the power of Christ may rest upon me.
2 Corinthians 12:9

...since you seek proof that Christ is speaking in me. He is not weak in dealing with you, but is powerful among you.
2

Corinthians 13:3

DEVOTIONAL 29: ASSAILED

Assailed. Tossed about. Worn and weary from the world. Have you ever felt something like that? It is comforting to me to know we are in good company.

In Luke 4:1-13, we see satan coming after Jesus with all the temptation and depletion techniques at his command. Jesus is in the wilderness for forty days. The word "wilderness" suggests a lack of water and other basic human comforts. He is in a dry place. Verse 2 states plainly that Jesus was hungry. It is in this empty, weakened state that His enemy comes at Him with a barrage of temptations. What did Jesus do? He responded every time with the Scripture that was so familiar to Him.

Jesus had also done one other thing that helped Him stand against the enemy: He lived in a state of readiness. Verse 1 says, *"Jesus, full of the Holy Spirit..."* When Jesus was ambushed, He was ready. His heart was full of the Holy Spirit and His mind was filled with Scriptures learned over His lifetime.

Why was He full of the Holy Spirit? If you look at the chapter just before this, you see Jesus going out to hear John preach and asking His cousin to baptize Him. Luke 3:21-22b reads:

21 Now when all the people were baptized, and when Jesus also had been baptized and was praying, the heavens were opened, 22 and the Holy Spirit descended on him in bodily form, like a dove;

Another important point in verse 21 is that Jesus was praying. Jesus was in the place the Father wanted Him to be; He was living in an attitude of prayer; and He was seeking all the Father had to give Him, no holding back.

So what happened in the end? Verse 13 reads:

And when the devil had ended every temptation, he departed from him until an opportune time.

That is a pattern I see happening so often with the devil. He assails and assails and assails, and finally he sees that a Christian is going to rely on the Lord and he just walks away. For a while. The end of verse 13 suggests the devil will be back at another time, but for now, he drops the assault of temptations. While you are being assailed, it seems to last forever and may seem your prayers are not being answered, but they are being heard. God is at work day and night to accomplish His purposes through you and to bless you, but the season of being assailed may seem almost unendurable.

Job went through this when satan dared God to let him put Job through trials that would wear him down to the point he would deny God *(Job 1.)* Satan attacked his property, killed his children, and finally left him miserable with sores all over his body, a weakened and miserable man. Despite all this, Job, though bewildered, sometimes hopeless, and crying out, did not turn against God.

So how did Job's season of being assailed end? God restored to him twice-over what he had before. His *"latter years were even better than his former years,"* but there was one more blessing that was the most wonderful of all. Job says to God in 42:5:

"I had heard of you by the hearing of the ear,
   but now my eye sees you;"

So when God ended this season, Job deeply knew his Heavenly Father in a way He had not known Him before his trials. Again, I see this happening in the Bible and in the lives of my friends who walk closely with the Lord like Job did. The sweet intimacy borne out of this type of suffering gives a depth to your relationship with the Lord that is costly but so worth it.

A final example of being assailed was when Satan asked to *"sift"* Simon Peter in Luke 22:32:

1 *"Simon, Simon, Satan has asked to sift all of you as wheat. 32 But I have prayed for you, Simon, that your faith may not fail. And when you have turned back, strengthen your brothers."*

And there ensued a night of temptation and failure on Peter's part that is painful to read about. Satan did not just tempt Peter once but three times before dawn, and he failed every test—that night. But what followed is the real story.

Jesus restored Peter, which he longs to do after we are tempted, whether we fail or prevail through Him. Jesus restores him so completely and magnanimously that shortly later, He says to Peter in Matthew 16:17-19:

17 *Jesus replied, "Blessed are you, Simon son of Jonah, for this was not revealed to you by flesh and blood, but by my Father in heaven. 18 And I tell you that you are Peter, and on this rock I will build my church, and the gates of Hades will not overcome it. 19 I will give you the keys of the kingdom of heaven; whatever you bind on earth will be bound in heaven, and whatever you loose on earth will be loosed in heaven."*

Jesus longs to restore you. He is well aware when you are being sifted. And you may experience difficulty after difficulty, setback after setback during that season as Jesus, Job, and Peter did. Being tested isn't a one and done deal; it is not a "yes" or "no" one-time pop quiz. Satan's tactic is to wear you down. During such a trial, you may even wonder if the Lord even sees you, knows what you are going through, and if your prayers are being heard. Be encouraged! Time after time we see God's children coming through these seasons of ordeal more blessed, more in love with Jesus, more richly enjoying the Holy Spirit, and more aware of the sovereignty and foresight of God. He will bring you through.

I wrote last week about being under attack. I understand that some do not like that term. Whether you call satan's ploys an attack, sifting, or a season of being assailed, we all know our God is greater and brings us through with His kind of victory every time, despite how dark the circumstances look.

I hesitated to write about this two weeks in a row, but some of the people I love best in this world are enduring such a season now. Maybe you are, too. I just wanted to say that you are in good company, and God will bring it to an end at the right time for His plan and for you. And you will come out the better for it. Like Jesus, stay in prayer, listening to the Word, and keep praising Him despite your emotions.

Luke 4:1-13 English Standard Version (ESV)   *4 And Jesus, full of the Holy Spirit, returned from the Jordan and was led by the Spirit in the wilderness 2 for forty days, being tempted by the devil. And he ate nothing during those days. And when they were ended, he was hungry. 3 The devil said to him, "If you are the Son of God, command this stone to become bread." 4 And Jesus answered him, "It is written, 'Man shall not live by bread alone.'" 5 And the devil took him up and showed him all the kingdoms of the world in a moment of time, 6 and said to him, "To you I will give all this authority and their glory, for it has been delivered to me, and I give it to whom I will. 7 If you, then, will worship me, it will all be yours." 8 And Jesus answered him, "It is written,*

"'You shall worship the Lord your God,
and him only shall you serve.'" 9 And he took him to Jerusalem and set him on the pinnacle of the temple and said to him, "If you are the Son of God, throw yourself down from here, 10 for it is written,

"'He will command his angels concerning you,
to guard you,'

11 and "'On their hands they will bear you up,
lest you strike your foot against a stone.'"

12 And Jesus answered him, "It is said, 'You shall not put the Lord your God to the test.'" *13* And when the devil had ended every temptation, he departed from him until an opportune time.

DEVOTIONAL 30: THE WIDE PLACE

"I shall walk in a wide place, for I have sought your precepts." Psalm 119:45

One thought from the Bible can always make me smile, relax, and say "ahhh." It is when I think about "The Wide Place." After a season of being assailed or harassed or tempted, God's inclination is to pluck you out of your difficulties and put your feet down in "The Wide Place." It is as if He says, "This is enough!" His compassion for us is so great that when His purposes are accomplished, it is not His wish to leave us in our suffering one minute longer than we need to.

Throughout the Bible, we see prophets and psalmists referring to this much longed for place of refreshment and restoration. Some versions call it the spacious, large, or broad place. I love 2 Samuel 22:20 especially because it points up the truth that God's placement of us in The Wide Place is unmerited and all for His own very personal reasons:

"He brought me out into a spacious place, he rescued me because he delighted in me."

Only God in His infinite mercy could find delight in His children like me who have rebelled repeatedly and failed to worship and follow Him with their whole hearts, but that is exactly what He does. He delights in us. That is a fact. He delights in me. He delights in you. Because of His personal delight in us, He wants to put us in The Wide Place.

Psalm 31:8 underscores that we cannot get into The Wide Place through our own efforts but that it is God who decides not to allow the enemy to overtake us, and it is God who sets our feet down there:

You have not handed me over to the enemy but have set my feet in a spacious place.

Psalm 118:5 NIV says that we should cry out to our loving Father when we are in distress:

When hard pressed, I cried to the Lord;
    he brought me into a spacious place.

And *Psalm 119:5* says we are to seek His precepts in His Word:

and I shall walk in a wide place, for I have sought your precepts.

Previously, we studied how Job was assailed. In *Job 30:15-16*, Job testifies to what he believes to be true of the Lord, despite the fact that his circumstances at the moment do not encourage Him to believe. He says:

"But those who suffer he delivers in their suffering; he speaks to them in their affliction. He is wooing you from the jaws of distress to a spacious place, free from restriction, to the comfort of your table laden with choice food."

I believe God is always wooing us from the jaws of distress and longing to restore us. I could go on with more Scripture, but you get my point.

So, what exactly is The Wide Place? The Wide Place is a rest stop on the very difficult journey a Christian has to walk. It is what R&R* is to a soldier who is pulled from the front lines of battle because his general knows that men need rest. It is similar to the player who is benched until he can get his breath and get back in the game with renewed vigor and zest for pressing hard toward the victory and the final buzzer.

One of the Hebrew words for The Wide Place is "ravach." It means "to breathe freely, to revive, to have ample room, to be refreshed."

One way I always know I am in The Wide Place is that I can breathe a bit easier; things just are not as hard every day. I feel I have more margin in my life, ample room just to live and not go relentlessly from one hard thing to the next.

When I am in The Wide Place, I always mention it to those around me and to groups I may be teaching. Because our hardships seem to draw the most attention, I want to point out this propensity God has for taking his people out of their hard circumstances and placing them in a roomy place with lots of space to breathe and stretch and enjoy Him.** He has a fondness for doing this, and that part of His nature does not get mentioned nearly enough. The best visual of it that I know is *Psalm 18:33 NASB*:

He makes my feet like hinds' feet, And sets me upon my high places.

The high places (this type) were places of safety and security. This place positioned the hind so he had an advantage over his enemies, above them looking down, and hard to reach. Just as Job testified above to the Lord's faithfulness during his horrendous circumstances, Habakkuk does the same thing in *Habakkuk 3:17*:

"Though the fig tree may not blossom, Nor fruit be on the vines; Though the labor of the olive may fail, And the fields yield no food; Though the flock may be cut off from the fold, And there be no herd in the stalls—Yet I will rejoice in the Lord, I will joy in the God of my salvation.

The Lord God is my strength; He will make my feet like deer's feet, And He will make me walk on my high hills." - HABAKKUK 3: 17-19 (NKJV)

Dear friend, when your circumstances are rocky, testify like Job and Habakkuk to the Lord's goodness and know that He will bring you into The Wide Place at the time that is best. And if you are in The Wide Place now, testify to others about His goodness. Encourage someone who needs to know that the Lord longs to bring them, too, into a place of rest, safety, and security.

*R&R is a military acronym for rest and recreation or recuperation.

**Some people fail to praise Him in difficult circumstances, but doing so is highly effective. Curiously, some people do praise Him in difficulty more than when they are in The Wide Place. Why would this be? For one thing, people desperate for God cry out and remember to speak of His attributes. They are in the foxhole. When they emerge from the foxhole and are no longer so desperate, the life they enjoy

114

may distract them from the impulse and need to meditate on His ways and praise Him. The Wide Place can be so enjoyable, we may not be in prayer as much as when we are being assailed at every turn. Don't let up just because you are enjoying life.

DEVOTIONAL 31: HIS POWER AND YOUR WORSHIP- STRENGTH FOR TODAY AND TOMORROW

We don't mean to sin. If I were to ask a large group of Christians if they could be assured they would never sin again, I believe they all would say, "Oh, yes, I want that very much."

But we find ourselves sinning again and again. Paul expressed this regret-filled condition this way:

"15 For I do not understand my own actions. For I do not do what I want, but I do the very thing I hate." Romans 7:15

God began perfecting us the day we accepted His free gift of salvation. Even though we sometimes feel this perfecting process is two steps forward and one step back, we can trust Him to complete the work that He began. Think about it. We may not trust ourselves, but Paul said in Philippians 1:6 that we could trust Christ because it is His work, after all:

And I am sure of this, that he who began a good work in you will bring it to completion at the day of Jesus Christ.

The sanctification process is going on in us daily because God loves us that much and wants to heal our sin-sickness. And we are better for it. More content for it. More fit for His use because of it. Every battle and trial we face is part of this process to strengthen us and make us more like Him. James 1:2-4 says:

2 Count it all joy, my brothers, when you meet trials of various kinds, 3 for you know that the testing of your faith produces steadfastness. 4 And let steadfastness have its full effect, that you may be perfect and complete, lacking in nothing.

The NIV version of verse four says:

Let perseverance finish its work so that you may be mature and complete, not lacking anything.

So the perseverance and endurance and steadfastness that are working in our imperfect souls and in our mistakes and in our circumstances are part of Christ working in us. It is not all on us.

So now that it is established that our sanctification is His work, let's look at one of the most effective things we can do to prepare our hearts and minds to accept His perfect work in us. I see this effective habit in the lives of so many people I admire.

Worship Him

Psalm 22:3 says:

Yet you are holy,
  enthroned on the praises of Israel.

In other words, God dwells in our praise. It is where He lives and can be found readily, consistently. Surround yourself with praise at all times because we never know what temptations and ambushes the day may hold for us, despite our good intentions. Starting the day in worship is especially effective. Being extra attentive to praising and worshiping Him grounds you in Him, reminds you of His identity and sovereignty, and allows you to rest in Him more easily. Soak yourself in His Words. Sing to Him and just talk to Him about His character and His great love for you. You will form a barrier against the enemy's attacks that cannot be pierced.

And if the attacks do come, fighting back with worship can send the enemy on the run. As you sing praise songs about how you love Him, that there is power in His blood, that He is a mighty fortress, and other truths that are in Bible-based music, your mind and heart are planted firmly and will not be easily moved to sin.

Be sure that the music you listen to is Biblically sound. Today, there is great emphasis on how Jesus can serve you to make your dreams come true. Some songs bring God down to our level. Be sure that the music you listen to and sing is true in every stanza about a God who is to be obeyed and adored, who loves you very much, but whose will is sovereign. Music should be God-centered and not me-centered.

I have had times when I was so grief-stricken or hurt that I could not think to sing. In those times, I have gotten out an old hymnal and feebly sung a song that is easy to remember. My voice is weak at first, but I find I get stronger as I sing each word. Or I sing a childhood song like *"Praise Him! Praise Him! All Ye Little Children."* If I truly cannot sing, I get out a few old CDs or download some songs that I know stir me to worship. I listen to the words and pray and agree with the singer as the song plays. Sometimes, if I am feeling dry, I will attend a hymn sing or worship time at another church that is holding a special night of praise.

Your worship can take many forms: prayer, song, art, or special love-gifts to acknowledge His goodness. Worship Him today to prepare your heart for whatever comes tomorrow.

DEVOTIONAL 32: STILLNESS by GUEST BLOGGER GLORIA POAGE

For the next four weeks, you will be treated to posts from some of my favorite people. Each guest blogger will bring something unique to the table. These are some true iron-sharpening-iron friends who strengthen me in the Lord. With these women, I always agree on the majors and can have some lively discussions on the minors when we disagree on theology, so I hope you will enjoy them as much as I do. We start with writer Gloria Poage whose bio is at the end of her blog.

Stillness

"Be still, and know that I am God. I will be exalted among the nations, I will be exalted in the earth." Psalm 46:10 ESV

Is stillness possible in this world of chaos, busyness, and division? We Christians are on a journey here on earth and, without a doubt, are affected by the demands of it. Our lives are filled with challenges beyond our ability to solve on our own. We need help! Ahh, and help is available.

Within the trustworthy pages of the Bible come the answers that lead to the Source who walks us through every challenge we face.

Being still before the Lord is an absolute necessity if peace and confidence are to enter our very spirit. We must make a conscious decision daily to feast on the Word of God for assurance of victory as we stand in the eye of life's storms.

Every living person is given 24 hours per day to do with it as they will. The world makes loud demands, but the Lord issues quiet invitations. The world's way brings confusion and loss, but God's way bears fruit of *love, joy, peace, longsuffering, gentleness, goodness, faith, meekness, and temperance. From Galatians 5:22-23.*

Physical food gives us energy for the body that satisfies until we get hungry again. More importantly, spiritual food brings lasting strength, not only for the day but for eternity!

By being still, reading the Word daily, and applying its principles, one day we will hear those awesome words – well done, good and faithful servant. It's our choice. Jesus is the Way, the Truth, and the Life, and no one is accepted by the Father except through Him.

Take advantage of this invitation, dear heart, as it brings joy in this world and bliss in Heaven to come.

About Gloria Poage

From early childhood, Gloria loved reading the Bible...the KJV! That developed a love for words that helped equip her for a thirty-four year career at Norfolk Southern Corp. (railroad), where she was given many assignments of writing and proofing.

She held a variety of offices in the church - one of the most special serving as a Sunday School teacher for thirty years to ten and eleven-year olds. According to Gloria, the teacher learned much!

Her love for the Lord grew stronger than ever in her retirement years, as she continued using her God-given gifts to His glory.

Gloria wrote this devotional shortly before she graduated and went to Heaven. We are grateful.

Gloria's radiant countenance and joy were a walking testimony to so many as she experienced intense and prolonged chemo for over a year. Her delight at the thought of living to serve Him here or at the prospect of joining Him soon were equal. She is one of the best examples to me of trusting the Lord completely with her future, even in her life or death circumstances.

DEVOTIONAL 33: GOD'S YES'S AND NO'S by CHARLOTTE TRAVIS

"For the Lord God is a sun and shield;

the Lord bestows favor and honor.

No good thing does he withhold

from those who walk uprightly."

Psalm 84:11

Today's guest blogger is Charlotte Travis. Charlotte is President of Abide in Him, Inc., whose mission is to strengthen the body of Christ through the teaching of God's Word. She enjoys teaching Bible Study and is the author of several verse-by-verse studies. A graduate of the University of Alabama and a former sixth-grade teacher, Charlotte is a wife and mother living in Kennesaw, Georgia. You can find the studies at www.AbideinHimInc.org or visit her blog at https://charlottetravis.wordpress.com.

I was talking with a neighbor when her son peeked out the door to find out more information about some cookies he found in the kitchen. His mother said they were left over from an event, and that he may have two. A spiritual analogy hit me later about God's yes's and no's. What if those cookies had been for an upcoming event? This loving and wise mother would have had to say, "You may have none." Does she love him more or less in either scenario? Of course not! God may at times allow us to have something we ask for, and at others times He may allow us to have none. We can be sure that a yes or a no is equally loving; for our good and His glory.

Psalm 84:11 holds a special place in my heart. During a hard season, it felt like God was holding out on me. I've learned that we can, and

121

must, take our hearts to Him no matter what shape they're in. With reverence, I was able to tell Him that I felt like He was holding out on me, but that I knew His Word is true, and He never withholds what is good from His children. The truth sets us free, and it does us good to bask in it.

We are blessed to be called to the family of God through Christ. No matter how we may feel, we can know He is our bright light and protection; always providing what is good. We may be allowed two or none, but either way we can be sure that He will never withhold what is good. His every move toward those in Christ is favor and honor, that others might be drawn to Him, too.

DEVOTIONAL 34: PRAYER by GUEST BLOGGER ANN KIEFFER

Today's guest blogger is prayer warrior Ann Kieffer. Ann was active in prayer at First Baptist Church Atlanta, the Atlanta Passion Play, and now at Church of the Apostles. She has prayed for many and has taught many to pray. She would often pray for total strangers who came to her estate sales for over forty years in her business, Exclusively 10 to 4. Ann is considering writing a book about prayer to share with even more people her ministry of prayer.

I read an article from TBN in which a lady mentioned "chatting with God." This brought to my mind the subject of prayer.

How personal is God to you when praying? Personal enough to …

Chat with?

Walk with?

Laugh with?

Be silent with?

Listen to?

Sing to?

Or is your fellowshipping with Jesus not so personal, but mainly …

Asking forgiveness?

Quoting Scriptures?

Giving praise?

Doing most of the talking?

Do you take the time to …

Sit with Jesus?

Be silent?

Let Him speak?

Do you ever laugh or is your conversation only serious? Do you ever serious?

Do you ever sing to Him even if you no longer can carry a tune?

Do you simply "chat?"

Do you share your secret feelings?

Do you tell Him a secret He already knows?

Do you give Jesus time for you two to walk in silence?

Do you feel you are here but the Lord is "way out there?" Remember, "He is a friend that is closer than a brother?"

Could there be a day Jesus wants someone to be with, and that someone is you?

Do you meet out of duty or performance? Out of a need you may have? Out of a question to be answered?

Or because of your relationship- a child and a Father? Two best friends- YOU! Whom He died for!!

"If you seek me you will find me."

Do you seek Him?

What do you say when you find Him?

Do you approach Him formally?

Or do you run into His outstretched arms?

You know God, you know Jesus, but do you know the Holy Spirit?

Do you know He has a sense of humor?

Do you know He loves to laugh?

Do you know He loves to hear about your day? (Although He already knows all about it!)

Do you know He wants to hear any serious concerns you have?

Do you go to the Trinity only when you have a serious problem?

Do you know He loves to just chat, as the lady said?

Do you know He loves to hear you say, "Father, do you know what happened to me today? Let me tell you." Of course, He knows- He orchestrated it, but He desires to hear about it from your mouth, your words, your heart, your experience! After all, His Word says, "Put me to remembrance." It's kind of like giving a child a gift. You know what it is; the thrill is seeing the child's excitement when opening it. God knows each gift given to you. It may be a gift of pain or sorrow or sickness. All God's gifts are not ones we want to open. But all bring us more into His image…

To bring Him the glory.

To fellowship in His sufferings.

To reflect His character in us.

Therefore, remember, prayer is *not* a formula, a list, a certain way.

No! Prayer is a conversation between two lovers! Our Creator created us to love and fellowship with Him.

You and I can enable this amazing oneness to take place if we take the time to be still and know He is God, God who desires to…

Walk with you.

Talk with you.

Listen to you.

Love you.

Laugh with you.

And at times, "chat" with you on this journey called life.

BONUS BLOG FROM ANN BELOW

Father, thank you for…

Allowing me to come to you

Blessing, me when I come to you

Comforting me

Delighting in me as your child

Enlightening me with your Word

Fighting for me against satan

Glorifying yourself in your Word

Holding me in prayer

Inviting me to pray

Judging me not!

Knowing you, just as I am

Loving me just as I am

Molding me in Your Image@

Near to me through the Holy Spirit

Oneness with me

Performing trough me (perfecting me)

Quiet within my soul

Resting in you- you in me

Studying your Word

Teaching me

Upholding me

Victory in Jesus

Winning with thee

X-ray in me – You know me inside

Yearning for you- through prayer and your Word

Zeal for you, Jesus

DEVOTIONAL 35: FROM AUTHOR OF JOY IN THE MOURNING

The blog below is an excerpt* from the upcoming sequel to **Joy in the Mourning***: Viewing the Rainbow from the Vale of Tears by Leslie Harder.* Joy in the Mourning *chronicles her first year as a bereaved mother and the lessons God taught her on her journey. Leslie's writing on grief has helped me frame things in my life of far less significance than her loss and her book has become my favorite gift to those who are grieving. She shares how God can redeem even the broken places in our lives and hearts and give us joy even in the midsl of great sorrow.* Joy in the Mourning *is available on Amazon. The author can be contacted at https://m.facebook.com/Psalm34Verse18/.*

Yesterday we began a new series in church on the Ten Commandments. Of course, the first message was about putting God first in everything in your life. One of the statements our speaker asked us to consider was this:

"If God is not first in my (fill in the blank), then God is not first in my life."

The speaker gave the examples that naturally come to mind: marriage, family, ministry. As he was speaking, one came to my mind that he probably never thought of.

If God is not first in my GRIEF, then God is not first in my life.

Wow. It stung a little bit to think of grief that way, but it is true. Grief is like having a ton of bricks thrown at you, sometimes in loads, sometimes one at a time. You may not have a choice about when it hits you or how hard, but you have a choice about what you do with it once it lands.

You can build a wall.

Or you can build a road.

You can wall yourself off from the comfort and presence of God and concentrate all your energies on that wall of grief, or you can pave a road--however hard it is or however long it takes--and choose to walk that road to the only Person who can truly bring you the comfort and peace you so desperately long for.

A wall.

Or a road.

It's up to you.

———————————

From <u>Through the Valley</u> by Leslie L. Harder. Used by permission.

Leslie's second book, a 60-day devotional entitled <u>Selah: 60 Moments with the Master</u> is slated for release on Amazon in October 2019.

DEVOTIONAL 36: LABOR DAY: YOUR WORK AS YOUR WITNESS

This blog is about Labor Day, but before you stay-at-home-moms, retirees, spouses who support the other spouse, and other non-traditional workers tune out, please hear me out. Some of you have much more challenging assignments than those who are blessed with a well-defined 9-to-5 job. Every Christian has assignments, laboring for the Lord in the home, the office, the school, or wherever. Our work is our testimony to so many people. How we do what we do reflects Jesus—or not. Before you think about standing up and giving a testimony, stop and review the testimony your everyday work on your assignment is giving people who may never read the Bible or go to church.

When I started my consulting practice teaching business communication skills to corporate employees, I wanted to commit my business to the Lord. Two verses guided every decision and influenced every work day.

The first is *Colossians 3:23:*

Whatever you do, work heartily, as for the Lord and not for men,

I love this verse, and it is a great plumb line to be sure you are working throughout the day in a Godly way that might make someone think highly of Christ-followers and therefore of Christ. Sadly, through my work for scores of companies through the years, I have heard complaints about a handful of Christians who are viewed as lazy or whose actions do not match the preachy words they profess in the workplace. If we are not authentic in what we believe or do not devote ourselves to reflecting well on the Lord in our neighborhoods and in our offices, people don't just make judgments about us; they make judgments about the one whose name we bear.

Colossians 3:23 energizes us to work, not as if we are working for our supervisor, VP, or company, but as if we are working directly for the Lord Himself. I assure you that if you go into your workplace or playgroup or construction site or housework with the Lord as your boss, the quality of your work and your productivity will go through the roof! Other versions of that verse tell us to work mightily, wholeheartedly, enthusiastically, willingly, cheerfully, or gladly. Some versions say do the best you can, do it from the heart, or to put yourself into it.

The second verse that guided my work was *I Timothy 5:18b.*

And, the laborer is worthy of his hire. ASV

Now I will admit that this verse was more about rewarding appropriately the leaders in the church, but as a very new Christian, I did not know that. I actually started my business, became a mom for the first time, and started following the Lord in the same year. There was a lot I did not know about all three of those things! Even though I did not understand the scope of that verse fully, the Lord still used it to guide me into serving my clients in a way that was different from other consultants, and He blessed the work of my hands.

I did know that this verse was more focused on telling others not to hold back appropriate rewards commensurate with the labors of the laborer. But the Lord impressed upon me that this was a two-way street. He convicted me that if I took a company's money, I should give them all the services, hours, and excellence due for the wages they gave me. And because I was a Christian, it was imperative I give beyond the basic amount due. No bare minimums for Christians. I knew that in business that often the customer and the service person have different expectations. Because my witness was more important than my bank account, I would have to go above and beyond what I thought was due at times in order not to damage my witness.

And this applies to excellence in all parts of our lives and all that we are in charge of. I had a neighbor recently who thought I should paint my house, even though it was not due. Another neighbor disagreed and felt I could wait a couple of years. What swayed me to do it was that my neighbor knows I am a Christian. The first neighbor's values say that every inch of your property should be perfect. I do not want something like a paint job damaging the name I bear as a Christian, and in this case, it would. They may never go to church with me, but they certainly watch how I live. They watch how I treat people and respond and listen. They observe if I get along *"as much as it is up to me."*

Enjoy the rest from your labors this Labor Day. Consider the verses below when you go back into the assignment God has given you for this season in your life:

If it is possible, as far as it depends on you, live at peace with everyone. Romans 12:18

And, the laborer is worthy of his hire. ASV I Timothy 5:18b

Whatever you do, work heartily, as for the Lord and not for men, Colossians 3:23

DEVOTIONAL 37: TAKING ON THE MIND OF CHRIST

A passage that helps me develop a Godlier-view of circumstances is Philippians 2:1-9.

So if there is any encouragement in Christ, any comfort from love, any participation in the Spirit, any affection and sympathy, ² complete my joy by being of the same mind, having the same love, being in full accord and of one mind. ³ Do nothing from selfish ambition or conceit, but in humility count others more significant than yourselves. ⁴ Let each of you look not only to his own interests, but also to the interests of others. ⁵ Have this mind among yourselves, which is yours in Christ Jesus, ⁶ who, though he was in the form of God, did not count equality with God a thing to be grasped, ⁷ but emptied himself, by taking the form of a servant, being born in the likeness of men. ⁸ And being found in human form, he humbled himself by becoming obedient to the point of death, even death on a cross. ⁹ Therefore God has highly exalted him and bestowed on him the name that is above every name,

The key verse here is verse 5 where we are encouraged to take on a mind like Christ. The NIV version says to *"Think of yourselves the way Christ Jesus thought of himself."* We should pray that every day we can take on more and more of Christ's ways of looking at our lives, circumstances, and most of all other people. Only when we are made whole in Heaven will we be able to do this with perfection, but hiding the Word in our hearts and staying in communication through prayer brings us closer to that ideal every day. Verses 2-4 make it clear that having the Christ-view of our circumstances means to be focused on others and not ourselves: *"⁴ Let each of you look not only to his own interests, but also to the interests of others."* When we really look at our circumstances with the interest of others uppermost, we can sometimes see why God is unfolding a plan for our lives that is quite different from what we selfishly had in mind. And sometimes, He is unfolding a plan for a sister or brother, and our lives are meant to play only a supporting role.

This mind is very different from the mind we naturally have. Each of us lives our lives as if it is a movie rolling to the end, and that we are the star, the protagonist, the action figure. *"Taking the form of a servant," "humbling ourselves,"* and *"becoming obedient to the point of death"* as Jesus did is counter to all human impulse and desire. But I have seen it time after time turn out to be a blessing to the servant as much as to the person being served when a friend sets aside self and *"counts others more significant than yourselves."*

God's purposes are God's purposes, and He will not let us decide how we are to be blessed in our lives. He decides how and when. But we know that no matter how counterintuitive it may be to sacrifice our will to do His will, that He will bless us in His way, the most perfect way. And He promises that good will result:

And we know that for those who love God all things work together for good, for those who are called according to his purpose. Romans 2:8

We do not have to wait to have the mind of Christ; it is ours to be enjoyed from the moment of our salvation. Verse 5 says, *"⁵ Have this mind among yourselves, which is yours in Christ Jesus."* We do not have to wait to mature or be taught; we can ask the Lord to give it to us now.

Even though Jesus was already perfect in every way, this passage tells us a couple of things He did when He walked this earth that we can use as our model. According to verses 7-8 above, He practiced the admonitions of these verses we have examined today. It was Jesus who *"emptied himself, by taking the form of a servant."* Truly emptying ourselves of Self with a capital "S" can be done only with the help of the Holy Spirit. Pray for His assistance and transforming power.

Secondly, Jesus *"humbled himself by becoming obedient to the point of death."* Examine your life. Is there a place where you are struggling to be obedient? Would you be obedient to the point of death?

Taking on the mind of Christ will change how you see others, will change your Christian walk, and will bring you greater peace and joy than you have ever had as you walk more closely and obediently with Him.

DEVOTIONAL 38: GOD'S SENSE OF HUMOR

When I was flailing around in sin and had no clue who God is, I think it would have made me want to know him more if someone had told me that God has a sense of humor. I thought of God as someone remote, living on a high and lofty mountain peak, and I never thought that a valley-dwelling sinner like me could ever relate to Him. I could conceive of a God who would spare me from His wrath or even pity me, but I could never have conceived of a God I could have a relationship with, a real and personal relationship. As I said, I think it would have helped.

Most of what I have learned about God's sense of humor is from my experience of walking with Him for the last thirty-plus years. He has given me a look at my own ridiculous self many times, and we have had a good laugh about some of my more embarrassing statements made with absolute confidence that I was right, like these examples:

1.The time my son asked if we could attend a church near his school, and I emphatically said I NEVER would (I have learned not to use that word "never" in earshot of God, who is everywhere.) I told my son that I drove to that intersection six times a week over forty minutes from our house, and I was NOT going to drive there on Sundays as well. Then I visited the church one time to check it out because he was planning on attending a church retreat there with a friend, and I joined the next Sunday. I have loved this church more than I could ever have imagined. I learned the meaning of Proverbs 16:9 NKJV:

A man's heart plans his way,
But the Lord directs his steps.

God always has the last laugh.

2. The many times I said I would NEVER write a blog :)

The Lord brings the counsel of the nations to nothing;
he frustrates the plans of the peoples. Psalm 33:10

But I also learned many lessons from the Bible, and the overall lesson is that laughter is a good thing. Psalm 17:22 says, *"A cheerful heart is good medicine, but a crushed spirit dries up the bones."* Another thing I learned is that it really depends on what is in your heart whether your laughter is good or bad, wise or foolish. For example, when Sarah first overheard she was going to have a baby in her old age, she laughed in disbelief or at least underestimation of what God can do. Genesis 18 says:

12 So Sarah laughed to herself, saying, "After I am worn out, and my lord is old, shall I have pleasure?" 13 The Lord said to Abraham, "Why did Sarah laugh and say, 'Shall I indeed bear a child, now that I am old?'14 Is anything too hard for the Lord? At the appointed time I will return to you, about this time next year, and Sarah shall have a son." 15 But Sarah denied it, saying, "I did not laugh," for she was afraid. He said, "No, but you did laugh."

But later, she laughed an entirely different type of laugh. She speaks of the laughter of joy related to what God undoubtedly did in her life. In other words Genesis 21:6 became her testimony of God's power and her absolute belief in His ability to do what He says He will do.

6 Sarah said, "God has brought me laughter, and everyone who hears about this will laugh with me."

Like Sarah, our joyous countenances and speech are often our most winsome testimony. Psalm 126:2 shows how God's people testify this way:

"Our mouths were filled with laughter, our tongues with songs of joy. Then it was said among the nations, "The LORD has done great things for them."

One of my favorite ways God displays His sense of humor or irony is in His conversations with people like Job, when He gives them a proper assessment of who they are and Who He Is. In short, with a few words, He puts them in their place. God does this in one of most beautiful passages in the Bible that starts in Job 38. Job has felt confident in his assumptions about God and how the world should work until God begins:

"Where were you when I laid the foundations of the earth?
Tell Me, if you have understanding.
5 *Who determined its measurements?*
Surely you know!" Job 38:4-5b

God goes on from there describing the wonders He has spun into place and asks Job where His part was in all this, clearly making Job see how ridiculous he has been.

I have had one of these, "Who do you think you are?" conversations with the Lord, and it is not fun, though I think we must be pretty comical to Him. One busy morning, I had a strong urging I was to witness to someone that day. I was reviewing all the people I would see that day and trying to get a clue from the Lord about which one He was trying to get me to engage with. When I came to one person, I quickly dismissed that person as someone who would never be interested in anything related to Christianity. Just as swiftly came the rebuke. I sensed God saying to me, "Who do you think you were when I found you?" When God turns the tables like this, we are convicted, sheepish, chastened, but purged. I had been this very person not so long ago. The irony was inescapable.

Corinthians 1:27 says, *"But God hath chosen the foolish things of the world to confound the wise; and God hath chosen the weak things of the world to confound the things which are mighty."* If we ever start thinking we are wise, He can make us see how foolish we really are. We become the buffoon in the joke when we are tempted to be prideful.

But after the chastening and the purging, God promises us that He Himself with fill us with joy and laughter. Job 8:21 says, *"He will yet fill your mouth with laughter and your lips with shouts of joy."*

And finally in Luke 6:21, Jesus leaves us with the promise that laughter is part of the future He has planned for us:

Blessed are you who hunger now, for you will be satisfied. Blessed are you who weep now, for you will laugh.

I look forward one day to sharing a laugh with the Lord, a good laugh when all my sin and time of chastening are in my past.

DEVOTIONAL 39: A TRUE FRIEND

Faithful are the wounds of a friend. Proverbs 27:6a

It is really hard to detect your own sin in its early stages. Sure, it is easy to see it when it blows up and becomes really ugly or when it results in consequences, which all sin eventually does. But how can we be more honest with ourselves when the first tendency toward sin begins to grow in our sin-sick hearts?

We cannot help our humanness, but sometimes a legitimate hurt can fester into sin. In other words, you can be perfectly innocent when someone hurts you for no reason. That hurt, however, can evolve into sin in your heart. If you nurse it, focus on it, resent it, avoid forgiving it, or do any number of other wrong things with it, the hurt can infect your heart with sin.

Our first response to someone hurting us is so important. We are not wrong to feel hurt. We were created with emotions for all kinds of sound reasons. So to hurt is human. What we want to do is to move as quickly as we can from our human response to a Christlike response. After all, we are daily trying to grow to be more like Him. Although we have seen it on a thousand posters and bracelets, the best response is to ask, "What would Jesus do?" and then follow His example. When He prayed for the people who were torturing and crucifying Him and said, *"Father, forgive them for they know not what they do,"* we were given a strong visual example of how we are to respond to being hurt.

In that moment, Jesus did not think of Himself; He thought of the people and the condition of their minds and hearts. If you are struggling to respond like Christ when people hurt you, this approach is an effective one. Stop and ask what is going on in the life and heart of the other person?

Someone once told me that at the basis of all anger is fear. When someone lashes out at me in anger, I first examine my own heart for sin. Next, I ask myself this about the angry person: "What are you so afraid of? How has what I have said or done made you feel threatened or defensive?" Stopping to consider what might be going on behind their eyes can help you change your response. It will help you do unto others as you would have them do to you because you have tried to put yourself in their shoes.

Another strategy to help you face your sin in an ongoing way is to develop accountability partners. We all need friends who will be honest with us about our sins. Most of our friends will be tempted to "take our side" in a conflict. A real Christian friend will be honest with you when you ask her to help you identify any sin you have in a situation.

The other night I was having dinner with some of my most delightful younger friends. The name of the counselor at our church came up, and we all agreed she is a wonderful Christian friend. I happened to say, "And what I like about her is that if I am wrong about something, she will not hesitate to tell me." I wish I could describe the look of shock on the young women's faces as they said, "She busts you?" I said, "Oh, ye-ah. She does not mind busting me at all."

They were thrilled! They said, "So you bust us, but she busts you?" I felt this should have been so obvious that I needed busting (to use their term) as much as they did, but they honestly had not realized that. It made them so happy that I told them that not only did *she* bust me but that our Director of Children's Ministries had busted me at one time, too, and it had been a good bust. A productive bust. A bust that resulted in my growth. That is what a real Christian friend will do for you.

And a good Christian friend will help you see your part in the creation or resolution of a problem. Even if the other person you are in conflict with has provoked the situation and sinned more than you have, you can probably identify something in your heart, words, or actions that could have been more Christlike. Ask the Holy Spirit and your Christian friend to help you identify your part. Don't let the other person's more obvious sin blind you to more subtle sins you have committed.

NOTE: Please consider this week whether you have Christian friends who do not just encourage you but also help you confront your sin. If you need strengthening in this area, please pray about it. You may need to ask God to send that type of Christian friend into your life. Or you may need to go to your Christian friends and give them permission to be more open with you about the sensitive topic of your sin.

Giving Your Friends Feedback

Another way to look at it is this. The original translation of the word sin was "to miss the mark." Not following Jesus or obeying Him is missing the mark. We can never attain perfection here on earth. From time to time, we all miss the mark. It reminds me of an exercise I once had my students do on communication. They had to get a rubber ball into a bowl. The problem was that they were blindfolded. They had a partner who could give them clues, but some partners were better than others. Some students struggled for far too long because their partners hesitated to tell them clearly when they were going wrong. Once they were off course, it was more difficult to get them back on track.

An interesting twist to this game was that at the beginning of the game, the partner was only allowed to tell the blindfolded students when they were doing something wrong. The blindfolded student only heard negative feedback. If he was on the right course and about to hit the mark, the partner could not encourage him and tell him he was doing well and should continue heading in the right direction. When partners were allowed to tell the blindfolded student when he was on the right track as well as when he was on the wrong track, the student got the ball into the bowl much faster. He was no longer missing the mark.

Being a good Christian friend is like that. You must tell your friend when she is weaving over the line into sin or even putting herself in a position to be vulnerable to sin. You must also tell her when she is on the right track and when you see her living for the Lord with passion and energy. Don't assume she already knows that. Everyone needs encouragement. The Christians around you need to hear your affirming words from time to time. Whom can you encourage this week?

DEVOTIONAL 40: THE BLESSING OF FRIENDSHIP

Oil and perfume make the heart glad, and the sweetness of a friend comes from his earnest counsel. Proverbs 27:9

Previously, we looked at how a true friend gives us honest counsel and acts as an accountability partner. But God had so much more in mind for us when He created this wonderful gift called friendship. I often think how generously and compassionately God was thinking the day He came up with the idea of friendship and decided we should have this blessing among all the other blessings He has given us.

It was God's idea that we should have a friend. We know this because He put into the minds of His handpicked authors to write verses about friendship throughout His Word. If you currently do not have a friend as you are reading this, be encouraged! We all have seasons of being friendless. I am praying for you today that God will soon introduce you to a Christian friend who will make these verses come true for you, too!

In Ecclesiastes 4:9-10, God makes it clear that He is in favor of friendship:

9 Two are better than one, because they have a good return for their labor:

10 If either of them falls down, one can help the other up. But pity anyone who falls and has no one to help them up.

A friend comes alongside us as and supports us in prayer, encouragement, and tangible action in all we undertake. I have just come from packing lunches for underprivileged children who lack the free school lunches in the summer that keep them going in the school year. One friend was supposed to lead this project, but she was called to a parent's sickbed in another state. She knew she could count on her friend to step in and help. That friend realized we needed more volunteers and called me. Because I am also a friend, I called my friends and soon we were abundantly staffed for the project. It was a lovely daisy chain of friends helping friends. We made over 300 sandwiches and bagged lunches today! To God be the glory!

A second thing a good Christian friend does is strengthen your hand in the Lord's. One of the most beautiful friendships in the Bible is that of David and Jonathan. At David's low point, he finds himself alone in the wilderness of Horesh. He is being pursued by King Saul and even being near the king brings danger. Despite that, Jonathan, Saul's son, goes to find David and to encourage him.

1 Samuel 23:16 says, *"And Jonathan, Saul's son, rose and went to David at Horesh, and strengthened his hand in God."*

What is interesting about this phrasing is that usually when the Bible mentions strengthening someone's arms or hands, it is God doing it. Since we seek to daily be more like our Lord, strengthening another's hand in the Lord's is demonstrating Christ-like behavior.

One way friends strengthen one another is through studying God's Word together. If you don't have a friend you can do this with, I encourage you to join a good Bible study where women get together to study His Word together. My friend Frances and I love getting together to get our nails done or to see a movie, but from time to time, we like to have God's Word be the focal point of our time together. We will go to a Christian bookstore and buy a Bible study book and do a study together for a few weeks, just the two of us. We both have family and church obligations, so we often cannot find a time to get together in person, but we will have an hour on the phone together on Saturday morning, sharing what we have learned from our study that week. It has strengthened both of us and strengthened our friendship. Over the last thirty years, we have been iron sharpening iron for each other:

17 As iron sharpens iron, so one person sharpens another. Psalm 27:17

Just this week, one of my favorite young friends, just weeks before her wedding, made time for her fiancé and her to take me out for a spiffy dinner. She endeared herself further to me during the meal when she lovingly and gently rebuked me for something I laughed at out of discomfort, yet should not have laughed at at all. Now that is a true friend.

Friends also pray for one another. I occasionally receive an email or text from a friend letting me know what God has put on their hearts to pray for me. These people are intercessors for me but they are also my friends, as is described in Job 16:20-21:

20 My intercessor is my friend as my eyes pour out tears to God;

21 on behalf of a man he pleads with God as one pleads for a friend.

In these verses, Job's earthly friends have let him down. It is the son of man who is interceding for Him. Earthly friends will let you down, even if they are good people. One key to long-term friendships is to accept this at the outset of any friendship, and remember His faithfulness during times when friends seem to be uncaring or insensitive to our pain. Because we always have the Son of Man as our intercessor as well as the Holy Spirit, all the pressure of intercession is not on our friends. We are never alone. We may be temporarily let down by even the best of earthly friends, but our friend and brother Jesus Christ never ceases praying for us.

I recently experienced nerve pain. Since it was not orthopedic but was invisible, some friends did not understand, but through it all, I knew that God knew all, saw all, and was compassionate about it all. We cannot expect friends who are human to understand all of our circumstances, and He assures us that we are never alone. I found this verse to be true in that difficult time:

…but there is a friend who sticks closer than a brother. Proverbs 18:24b

We can enjoy our earthly friends, grow in the Lord with our friends, and serve the Lord with them, but it is wonderful to know that the Lord also wants to be our friend. He considered it important for us to know that He did not just look at us as subjects and servants—He looks at us as friends!

12 My command is this: Love each other as I have loved you.

13 Greater love has no one than this: to lay down one's life for one's friends.

14 You are my friends if you do what I command.

15 I no longer call you servants, because a servant does not know his master's business. Instead, I have called you friends, for everything that I learned from my Father I have made known to you.

John 15:12-15

Talk to the Lord today about His offer of friendship to you and how you feel about it. And if you are in need of a friend who will be iron sharpening iron in your life, ask yourself if you are putting yourself in Bible studies, small groups, and events that would offer opportunities for conversations that might lead to Godly friendship.

Additionally, I have made some of my best lifelong friends through service projects. Serving together is a wonderful way to get to know someone. Also ask yourself if you are limiting God in your narrow view of who might be your friend. Two of my closest friends are twenty years my senior, and they are fun, wise women. One great way to find a friend is to be a friend to someone who is in need.

Finally, the best way to find a Godly friend is to pray and ask God to send that person into your life in His way and in His time. In the meantime, enjoy the blessing of lots of time alone with the *"friend who sticks closer than a brother."*

DEVOTIONAL 41: DON'T GO OUT UNARMED

This week's blog gives you a glimpse into the lives of three mighty women of God and how they prepare for the battle against sin in different ways.

I Peter 4:12 is a very strategic verse for fighting sin:

Since therefore Christ suffered in the flesh,
arm yourselves with the same way
of thinking, for whoever has suffered in the flesh has ceased from
sin, 2 so as to live for the rest of time in the flesh
no longer for human passions but for the will of God.

I Peter 4:1, tells us that Christ Himself suffered in the flesh and that we should prepare by arming ourselves with (His) same way of thinking. The second part of this verse links changing our thinking to ceasing from sin. I have had three wise women in my life who have had three very different approaches to arming themselves against temptation. All of these approaches are effective and worthy of emulating.

The first woman depends on Ephesians 6:13-18 that tells us to put on the whole armor of God:

13 Therefore take up the whole armor of God, that you may be able to withstand in the evil day, and having done all, to stand firm. 14 Stand therefore, having fastened on the belt of truth, and having put on the breastplate of righteousness, 15 and, as shoes for your feet, having put on the readiness given by the gospel of peace. 16 In all circumstances take up the shield of faith, with which you can extinguish all the flaming darts of the evil one; 17 and take the helmet of salvation, and the sword of the Spirit, which is the word of God, 18 praying at all times in the Spirit, with all prayer and supplication.

My friend Ann Kieffer, for many years, would rise every morning and literally dress herself with each part of the armor. Friends on a beach trip with her said they saw her rise early and go outside to pray, carefully fastening a belt they could not see, putting on shoes invisible to them, and carefully adjusting the helmet of salvation on her beautiful, sweet head. Before you think this is going too far, think about how aware she was of the truth, the gospel of peace, and the protection of her salvation as she made herself conscious of each one as she put them on every morning. If you know her, you know that God's protection has been strong over her life. I can't help but believe that this practice had much to do with it. Her willingness to take the Bible literally and to submit herself to an exercise that might look over the top to others may just be why God has been able to use her mightily in so many people's lives as a prayer warrior. I know He has used her in mine.

Another friend has a quite different approach. Julie Van Gorp is co-founder of TrueViewMinistries.org, a wonderful ministry that helps women live without fear as they engage in a Christlike manner with our culture. She has a practice that may seem extreme when I first describe it. She told me once that when I had difficulty letting go of something, I should be dead to it. Now I had read many verses about dying to my selfish desires, to self in general, and to sin, so I complacently agreed. She said, "No, I mean really dead, like you are in a coffin. If you are dead to something, truly dead, you cannot feel it at all. The things that are bothering you today will not have any effect on you when you are dead and in your coffin."

It was hard to argue with that, but it is more difficult than you think to be truly dead to resentment, jealousy, anger, or hurt. When I thought about the day I would someday be truly dead, I saw that she was right that these petty matters would not have any pull on me. I wanted to be dead to them now. And the Bible offers ample Biblical support for this thinking:

Romans 6:11 *So you also must consider yourselves dead to sin and alive to God in Christ Jesus.*
Romans 6:2
By no means! How can we who died to sin still live in it?
Romans 6:7 *For one who has died has been set free from sin.*
Galatians 5:24
And those who belong to Christ Jesus have crucified the flesh with i ts passions and desires.

Colossians 3:3
For you have died, and your life is hidden with Christ in God.
Colossians 3:5 *Put to death therefore what is earthly in you:*
sexual immorality, impurity,passion, evil desire, and covetousness,
which is idolatry.

Another example to me is my friend and long-time Bible teacher Carolyn. From Carolyn, I have learned two things: the Biblical view of authority and what Jesus meant when He talked about having the faith of a little child.

Carolyn's global travel and her background in art history have given her more than the usual insight into what certain Scriptures mean. She has taught me to try to understand the context of what is going on in a passage and to understand the culture of the characters in familiar Bible stories. She brought these alive to me in our 6:45AM Bible study that I attended for fifteen years.

But Carolyn's unique impact on women has been in modeling how to live joyously as a woman today while observing the Biblical principles of authority. Her respect and admiration for her husband was always evident whenever she spoke of Him, and he was one of the wisest and most compassionate men I have ever known. She would quote his advice and say, "Jimmy says…" In much the same way, when she would look for wisdom in the Bible, she would say, "Jesus says….," with the same admiration, love, and childlike faith. And she has so much wisdom because of her reliance on Him and His Word.

The final example in my life for battling sin effectively is my mentor and first Bible teacher, Frances. She does not have a formula, and her advice has only been in the form of the example she is to me. We have walked side by side through blessings and tragedies, in times of peace and times of great attack from the world for thirty years. I can tell you that she consistently walks this earth following the example of Jesus Christ. The way we all aspire to respond to sin and to others is the way I see her responding day after day, year after year. When I try to come up with a reason her walk is so different from even most Christians', I think of two things about her. First, Frances has a passion for purity and piety. She is consumed with the desire to understand these things better and has studied her Bible for decades to search what those words mean and how to accept them into her life. She is not doing this to teach a class or to appear saintly. She really wants to know about these attributes because she knows the Lord loves them. In this moment, you may have an image of Frances as being distant from her fellow sinners or holier than thou. Nothing could be further from the truth about this humble, unpretentious, fun-loving woman. She has blinders on to what others are doing wrong and concerns herself with the condition of her own soul. Hers is not an "I want to be better than my peers" pursuit of piety. Her eyes are only on Jesus and wanting to please Him. As she studies the words in her Bible and in the writings of Biblical teachers throughout the years, her walk is influenced by what she is pouring into her mind.

The second thing about Frances is that prayer and the Bible are her first responses to anything—good or bad. When something disappointing happens, her first line of defense is not to go tell everyone or to seek worldly solutions. You will find her taking the key words of the situation and scouring her Bible and praying. She gets alone with God, and the two of them have wonderful fellowship, even if what has driven her there is not wonderful.

And she prays constantly in private and in corporate prayer. It is tempting when we are mistreated or disappointed to talk and talk about our problems, but the bulk of Frances' talk is just to the Lord. I am still learning from her.

What does this mean to you, to *"arm yourself with the same way of thinking"* as I Peter 4:1 says? Do you have your own go-to verses or approach? Would experimenting with one of the above strengthen you? To help you answer these questions, below are other Scriptures about ceasing from sin:

Romans 6:14
For sin will have no dominion over you, since you are not under law but under grace.

James 4:7 *Submit yourselves therefore to God. Resist the devil, and he will flee from you.*

DEVOTIONAL 42: A WEEK OF ADORATION

I thought it might be good to take a day just for adoration. Let's pause a moment and contemplate how glorious, how holy, and how lovely our Father is, our Lord is, and the Holy Spirit is. This blessed Trinity has been blessing us since before we were born, and a pause to praise them is more than due. I invite you to share your praise or a verse that expresses praise, awe, or wonder at Who He is.

Below are three of my favorite Bible passages that touch on His transcendent glory, might, majesty, and power. I am staggered that the Lord has made all of that available to me to bless me and operate in my life today, and not just in Heaven. One of the things nonChristians express to me after reading my first book is that they did not know that God could operate in such a personal way in today's times. Yes!! That is part of the Good News. The verses below honor, worship, and acknowledge Who He is!

He is the radiance of the glory of God and the exact imprint of his nature, and He upholds the universe by the word of his power. After making purification for sins, he sat down at the right hand of the Majesty on high,

Hebrews 1:3

He heals the brokenhearted
  and binds up their wounds.
4 He determines the number of the stars
  and calls them each by name.
5 Great is our Lord and mighty in power;
  his understanding has no limit.
6 The Lord sustains the humble
  but casts the wicked to the ground.

7 Sing to the Lord with grateful praise;
make music to our God on the harp.

8 He covers the sky with clouds;
he supplies the earth with rain
and makes grass grow on the hills.
9 He provides food for the cattle
and for the young ravens when they call.

10 His pleasure is not in the strength of the horse,
nor his delight in the legs of the warrior;
11 the Lord delights in those who fear him,
who put their hope in his unfailing love.

12 Extol the Lord, Jerusalem;
praise your God, Zion.

13 He strengthens the bars of your gates
and blesses your people within you.
14 He grants peace to your borders
and satisfies you with the finest of wheat.

15 He sends his command to the earth;
his word runs swiftly.
16 He spreads the snow like wool
and scatters the frost like ashes. Psalm 147

And I love God's response when Job presses for an answer to why he has suffered. God lets Job know who He is by questioning Job about who he is (emphasis on lower-case "h.")

The word "awesome" should be reserved for the awe we can feel for the astounding creative and dynamic reach of God Almighty. If we can just for a moment grasp what the following verses say, we should be truly awed by the stunning acts of art, science, physics, and humanity that our Father sets in motion every day that reveal just a glimmer of His power:

"Where were you when I laid the earth's foundation?
  Tell me, if you understand.
5 *Who marked off its dimensions? Surely you know!*
  Who stretched a measuring line across it?
6 *On what were its footings set,*
  or who laid its cornerstone—
7 *while the morning stars sang together*
  and all the angels[a] shouted for joy?

8 *"Who shut up the sea behind doors*
  when it burst forth from the womb,
9 *when I made the clouds its garment*
  and wrapped it in thick darkness,
10 *when I fixed limits for it*
  and set its doors and bars in place,
11 *when I said, 'This far you may come and no farther;*
  here is where your proud waves halt'?

12 *"Have you ever given orders to the morning,*
  or shown the dawn its place,
13 *that it might take the earth by the edges*
  and shake the wicked out of it?
14 *The earth takes shape like clay under a seal;*
  its features stand out like those of a garment.
15 *The wicked are denied their light,*
  and their upraised arm is broken.

16 *"Have you journeyed to the springs of the sea*
  or walked in the recesses of the deep?
17 *Have the gates of death been shown to you?*
  Have you seen the gates of the deepest darkness?
18 *Have you comprehended the vast expanses of the earth?*
  Tell me, if you know all this.

19 *"What is the way to the abode of light?*
    And where does darkness reside?
20 *Can you take them to their places?*
    Do you know the paths to their dwellings?
21 *Surely you know, for you were already born!*
    You have lived so many years!

22 *"Have you entered the storehouses of the snow*
    or seen the storehouses of the hail,
23 *which I reserve for times of trouble,*
    for days of war and battle?
24 *What is the way to the place where the lightning is dispersed,*
    or the place where the east winds are scattered over the earth?
25 *Who cuts a channel for the torrents of rain,*
    and a path for the thunderstorm,
26 *to water a land where no one lives,*
    an uninhabited desert,
27 *to satisfy a desolate wasteland*
    and make it sprout with grass?
28 *Does the rain have a father?*
    Who fathers the drops of dew?
29 *From whose womb comes the ice?*
    Who gives birth to the frost from the heavens
30 *when the waters become hard as stone,*
    when the surface of the deep is frozen?   Job 38:4-30*

 The entire chapter of Job 4 contains a series of these questions that give Job and us just a glimpse of His awesome power, divine discretion, and ways so far above our ways we can barely glimpse them in our clay-like state of being mortal.

What about you? What verses or observations move you when you think about our awesome God?

DEVOTIONAL 43: PLAYING YOUR LYRE FOR YOUR ENEMY

I will also praise You with a harp, Even Your truth, O my God; To You I will sing praises with the lyre, O Holy One of Israel. Psalm 71:22

What if someone were jealous of you to the point of reading wrong motives into everything you did? What if this person, your declared enemy, asked you to serve him or her in many ways? And how would you feel after you did every act of service requested in a sacrificial and generous way, but your enemy hated you even more for fulfilling the requests? What would be your response? Would you try to give him (or her) moments of beauty and peace and relief from his pain?

Because that is what David did for King Saul.

From the time David was a young boy, all he ever wanted to do for Saul was to serve him and bless him. At various times, David served as a personal musician, as the equipment manager for Saul's troops, and as the most effective soldier in Saul's army. Whatever Saul asked David to do, David put forth extraordinary effort and prayer to exceed Saul's expectations. And therein lay the problem. Even though David only meant good toward Saul, the very excellence in David's efforts incensed Saul and incited the king's jealousy further.

Saul threw spears at the young man, gave orders to have others kill him, and banished him from his kingdom so that David had to leave his home and family and all that was familiar. Saul stripped David of all he had in return for the young man's doing everything in his power to demonstrate his love, loyalty, and desire to please.

So what did David do? He continued to risk his life for Saul over and over again. When he was in Saul's courts, he played the most beautiful music of any of Saul's musicians in an effort to comfort the king and to give him peace. When the evil but brilliant Doeg told lies about David, the king never took a minute to consider David's track record but immediately believed the gossip. Saul really needed no excuse to believe the worst of David, so the king drove him away from his native land. The hardest part for David was being driven away from the temple and the religious life of his community, a great loss to a man who loved the Lord with all his heart. It was during one of the times of being on the run that David said the words in Psalm 120:5:

Woe is me, for I sojourn in Meshech, For I dwell among the tents of Kedar! NASB

Matthew Poole in his commentary paraphrases David's lament this way:

"Let us weep, because in this life we are forced to sit by the waters of Babylon, and are yet strangers and as it were banished and barred from being satisfied with the pleasures of that river which gladdens the city of God. Alas, if we did consider that our country were heaven, and did apprehend this place here below to be our prison, or place of banishment, the least absence from our country would draw tears from our eyes and sighs from our hearts, with David *(Psalms 120:5)*:"

David, on the run and hunted as prey by Saul, had ample opportunity to end his banishment and persecution by ridding himself of this enemy Saul, yet opted to demonstrate his love and mercy to Saul time after time. Once when Saul took three-thousand men to pursue and kill David, the king left himself in a vulnerable position while relieving himself in a cave. David could have easily escaped a future of having a price on his head, but instead he cut off a piece of Saul's cloak to demonstrate what he *could have done* if he had so chosen. David says to his murderous pursuer:

"12 May the LORD judge between you and me. And may the LORD avenge the wrongs you have done to me, but my hand will not touch you." I Samuel 24:12

This episode ends with David giving Saul an assurance he will never wipe away the king's descendants from the earth. That is what David gives his enemy instead of what Saul richly deserves.

Although Psalm 137 is about being taken captive by the Babylonians, the doleful yearning to be restored to home is timeless for God's people. One of the most poignant scenes in the Bible for me is when the captives have been in bondage for some time and are asked to sing the songs of their native Zion for their captives.[1] These are the holy songs, songs meant for reverent worship and not for the entertainment of the hedonistic Babylonians. At some point the captives cannot go on, and in grief and sorrow hang their harps on the trees by the river. They sit, which is a posture of dejection and futility. Psalm 137:1-4 portrays this heartbreaking scene.

By the rivers of Babylon we sat and wept
    when we remembered Zion.
² There on the poplars
    we hung our harps,
³ for there our captors asked us for songs,
    our tormentors demanded songs of joy;
    they said, "Sing us one of the songs of Zion!"
⁴ How can we sing the songs of the LORD
    while in a foreign land?

There are scholars who believe that not singing for their captors was the right thing to do, but remember that Jeremiah had told them to make the best of the situation in their new land, to build homes, and have children. Who knows how winsome the songs of Zion may have been to at least some of the Babylonians? In the history of God's people, those who did serve their captors, Daniel and Nehemiah in particular, were able to do great things for God's people and to bring Him much glory.

Often in life, God asks us to be like David. He asks us not just to grit our teeth and endure those who persecute or challenge us; He asks us to pick up our harps and let them hear the music of Heaven through us. Few of us can play musical instruments, but all of us can be played like an instrument in God's hands. Your soft response to a snappy neighbor or to a boss who is treating you unfairly may be a chord of a different kind of song their ears have never heard. Instead of hitting a wrong note, your refusal to demand your rights may make a pleasant sounding note in their ears, a refreshing song compared to the blaring cacophony they usually hear all day long.

The next time someone comes against you and you are undeserving of their unkindness, pick up your harp. You may feel dejected or angry, but demonstrate the harmonious and beautiful song God put in your heart the day you were saved.

It is good to give thanks to the LORD And to sing praises to Your name, O Most High; To declare Your lovingkindness in the morning And Your faithfulness by night, With the ten-stringed lute and with the harp, With resounding music upon the lyre. Psalm 92:1-4

DEVOTIONAL 44: UZZIAH, STRONG AND PROUD

I wish the times of walking closely in tandem with the Lord would carry over continuously year after year, day after day for me. I wish that once I learned a lesson through His Word and through the Holy Spirit teaching me that I would never have weak moments when I lapse into old impulses, old ways of thinking, or old fears. And though I know that salvation, my eternal spot in Heaven, and all good things are simply gifts from His hand, I still find myself acting as though I wish my good performance counted for something. When I say something thoughtless that is not glorifying to Him, I can still have that momentary thought, "Lord, you know I am not usually like this. I hope yesterday's performance counts in my favor." Yes, I know that this is not how Grace works, but years of performance-based living sometimes makes me forget for a moment that His blood washes away my current sin completely. For a millisecond, I forget that nothing I have done can add to or subtract from His Grace. But then I remember with gratitude that truly, His mercies are new every morning.

I have a great deal of empathy for Uzziah (783-742 BC) and his failures but consider these things you may not know about him. He was tutored by the prophet Zechariah and was faithful to God for over five decades. Consider how faithfully Uzziah followed hard after the Lord and lived to give God glory. Below is just a partial list from 2 Chronicles 26 of all Uzziah accomplished because he let the Lord use him:

· He was sixteen years old when he became King of Judah, with the support of "*all the people.*"

· His 52-year reign was one of the most prosperous since the time of Solomon.

· "*He did what was right in the eyes of the Lord.*"

· "*He set himself to seek God in the days of Zechariah, who instructed him in the fear of God.*"

159

·   He commanded an army of 307,000, made war on the Philistines, restored cities to Judah, and built new cities.

·   *"The Ammonites paid tribute to Uzziah, and his fame spread even to the border of Egypt, for he became very strong. **9** Moreover, Uzziah built towers in Jerusalem at the Corner Gate and at the Valley Gate and at the Angle, and fortified them. **10** And he built towers in the wilderness and cut out many cisterns, for he had large herds, both in the Shephelah and in the plain, and he had farmers and vinedressers in the hills and in the fertile lands, for he loved the soil."*

Uzziah was God's man. As a young man, he had humbly taken instruction from a man of God who truly understood God's will and God's way. He acknowledged God in all he did. He loved God's house and he loved to worship Him. So what happened?

In 2 Chronicles 26:5 we read some ominous words:

He set himself to seek God in the days of Zechariah, who instructed him in the fear of God, and <u>as long as he sought the Lord</u>, God made him prosper.

Those words "<u>as long as he sought the Lord</u>" compose an important clause. Everything in Uzziah's future hinges on those seven words.

Similarly, 2 Chronicles 26:5 hints at things to come:

And his fame spread far, for he was marvelously helped, <u>till he was strong</u>.

Finally, verse 16 tells us why Uzziah's life of victory through the Lord is about to take a hard left into misery and humiliation:

<u>But when he was strong</u>, he grew proud, to his destruction. For he was unfaithful to the Lord his God and entered the temple of the Lord to burn incense on the altar of incense.

160

Did he derail when he was weak? Not it was "*when he was strong*!" Was he unfaithful to the Lord because he stopped going to God's house and serving the Lord? No, his downfall came when he "*entered the temple of the Lord.*"

Uzziah's story is one every mature Christian and servant of the Lord should revisit regularly. How easily we can feel we are "strong." How easily we can be so familiar with church work and the Bible that we fail to consult the Lord in stillness and earnest prayer to seek His will. Any time our service becomes business as usual and we lose that feeling that we are hanging on God's every word to tell us what to do next, we should take a step back. We should always feel that God is a step ahead of us and we are gripping the hem of His cloak saying, "Wait, God, wait. Tell me what you want. What is next? How do you see this? Should I go left or right? Swing or take the ball?"

Even if we have seen a situation a dozen times in our service to Him and feel our experience should teach us exactly what to do, we should enter each fresh act of service with supplication that we will not make a move without waiting for a nudge, a word, or direction from Him. There are no professional Christians. Each day, we start with those fresh mercies. And each day, God may be about to do something totally new, something you have never seen Him do in your life. You cannot rely on your experience which is yours and not His. He is all you can rely on. It is exciting, but it is like getting on a roller coaster each day for the ride of your life. Be submissive to all the bends, turns, and heart-in-your throat moments in the ride He has chosen for you.

Uzziah's problem was not that he would not serve the Lord. His problem was that He wanted to serve the Lord his way. He only wanted to be obedient in his sacrifice in a way that spotlighted him at the center of the worship. *"He grew proud, to his destruction. For he was unfaithful to the Lord his God and entered the temple of the Lord to burn incense on the altar of incense."* He was struck immediately with leprosy and never recovered. Even God's children with the greatest track records for service do not get the day off from obedience. No matter how well we know the Lord, we still have to consult with Him, because He deals so differently with each of His children and may take us in directions we would never have predicted.

We are now under the new Covenant where Grace and mercy abound, but the Lord still loves us enough to ask for our obedience—for our own good and for His ultimate glory. And there still may be temporary, earthly consequences to our disobedience, even though He does His best to protect us and guide us away from our rebellious choices.

If Uzziah had taken only a moment to consult the Lord and His Word, he would have remembered that God had been clear that only the priests and not the king should enter the temple to burn the incense. But Uzziah did not slow down to prayerfully consider what the Lord wanted. He rushed into an act of worship and service just assuming that he had a very good idea for what his sacrifice should look like. Have you ever done that- rushed into an act of service without covering it in prayer and waiting to consider what the Lord actually wanted from you? I certainly have.

Burning the incense was an act of worship but it was not an act of obedience. I Samuel 15:22 says:

And Samuel said, "Has the LORD as great delight in burnt offerings and sacrifices, as in obeying the voice of the LORD? Behold, to obey is better than sacrifice, and to listen than the fat of rams."

Prayerfully consider this verse the next time you rush into an act of service or take off in a new direction. As much as you think your plan to serve Him is a great idea, make sure it is actually His idea and not your own. And if you need friends to come alongside you to seek His will, that is a strength and not a weakness.

DEVOTIONAL 45: NO NEED TO BE CAREFUL

I read a passage recently that knocked me back for a moment. It went against a lifetime of habit, indoctrination, and mindset. Read this and see if anything in it shocks you the way it shocked me:

Blessed is the man that trusteth in the LORD, and whose hope the LORD is. For he shall be as a tree planted by the waters, and that spreadeth out her roots by the river, and shall not see when heat cometh, but her leaf shall be green; and shall not be careful in the year of drought, neither shall cease from yielding fruit. Jeremiah 17:7-8 KJV

What? Not be careful in the year of drought? I am always careful. I have spent my life preparing for times of drought. Can the Bible really be saying not to be careful in the dry times?

You may not be knocked for a loop by this verse the way I was. Let me explain how I got this way. I was raised by parents who were deeply affected by The Great Depression, and at our house, we lived as if we were always preparing for the inevitable next Great Depression. My Dad was a wonderful provider and over-insured us for everything, and as an adult, I have over-insured myself for any possible disaster ever since I was old enough to purchase insurance. I have held the maximum long-term care disability insurance available since I was in my thirties (I am saying this with embarrassment)! As a single mom, I wanted to be sure I was not a burden to my family and that all the details of my care were provided for. This is my mentality. At the root of it is fear. Also, it indicates the belief in self and a worship of self-reliance that has been a scourge in my spiritual growth for all of my adult life. It is a pride issue that I must face and fight over and over again.

The Lord does not want me to be self-reliant. He wants me to rely on Him. He wants me to have confidence in Him and not myself. Here are some things He has told me in His Word about where my confidence should lie:

- *For the LORD will be your confidence and will keep your foot from being caught. Proverbs 3:26*

- *In the fear of the LORD one has strong confidence, and his children will have a refuge. Proverbs 14:26*
- *Such is the confidence that we have through Christ toward God. [5] Not that we are sufficient in ourselves to claim anything as coming from us, but our sufficiency is from God, 2 Corinthians 3:4*
- *So we can confidently say, "The Lord is my helper; I will not fear; what can man do to me?" Hebrews 13:6*

And the Lord tells me clearly that I am not to try to take care of my own future through self-reliance or fear or worry:

- *For we are the circumcision, who worship by the Spirit of God and glory in Christ Jesus and put no confidence in the flesh— Philippians 3:3*

In fact, He tells me very plainly not to lean on my own intellect and self-direction:

- *Trust in the LORD with all your heart, and do not lean on your own understanding. In all your ways acknowledge him, and he will make straight your paths. Proverbs 3:5-6*

He warns me that my confidence is in the Lord and not myself, and to take great care not to throw this true and reliable confidence away by switching my trust to self-confidence as the world encourages me to do:

- *Therefore do not throw away your confidence, which has a great reward. For you have need of endurance, so that when you have done the will of God you may receive what is promised. Hebrews 10:35-36*

He tells me honestly in I Timothy 3-4 that very difficult times will arise for me, so the things I worry about are real things. The drought Jeremiah referred to in my life can be a drought of love, or financial security, or anything else I might fear being deprived of, but that if I place my confidence in Him and not in myself or other humans, He states strongly that He is more than capable of conquering anything that comes my way:

- *Though an army encamp against me, my heart shall not fear; though war arise against me, yet I will be confident. Psalm 27:3*
- *Fear not, for I am with you; be not dismayed, for I am your God; I will strengthen you, I will help you, I will uphold you with my righteous right hand. Isaiah 41:10*
- *And this is the confidence that we have toward him, that if we ask anything according to his will he hears us. 1 John 5:14*

Finally, He has given me this go-to verse when my thinking gets all askew about the One who truly can protect me and Who has the ability to do unimaginable and victorious things to deliver me from any troubles:

- *What then shall we say to these things? If God is for us, who can be against us? Romans 8:31*

When I am feeling overwhelmed with pressure, worry, fear of the unknowns in my future, or am just too much in my head, I think of this verse and almost laugh out loud. The idea of any foe I might think I have here on this earth, up against the Almighty God of the universe, the Creator of mountains, oceans, and deep space, the designer of everything, and Who has angels and all the earth at His command, well, it is just laughable to think I should be worried for even a minute. My confidence is in the Lord.

DEVOTIONAL 46: KEEP YOUR CHANNELS CLEAR

But seek first the kingdom of God and his righteousness, and all these things will be added to you. Matthew 6:33

Communication has changed so much since I was a child growing up in Texas in the '50s. If a phone call were very important to my mother, she would be sure not to accept any other calls all day as she waited for that special call. Or she would answer and say, "I have to get off this phone. So-and-so (usually someone in her family from Georgia) said she would call today. I have to keep the line clear." It was not that the other calls were not important to her, but a call from her mother was a call she would prioritize over everyone and everything.

Naturally, this was before caller id and call waiting. We had to make choices in those days if we truly valued a call and were willing to put that special person ahead of everything else.

Prayer is like that. With our busy lives, prayer does not happen without some intentionality. The old saying that "the good is the enemy of the best" is more true for Christians than for anyone. There are so many good things we can do with our time. There are so many Godly people we can talk to who would be edifying. There are so many in need we could be serving and talking to. But if we do not keep the line clear for the Lord Himself to communicate with us, our prayer life can be haphazard and not as deep and rich as we want it to be. If we really want to experience the Lord fully in His power and majesty and we want to receive His direction in an effective way, we will have to make time for it.

You shall have no other gods before me. Exodus 20:3

I think of God as the ultimate CEO of the world. If in my business, a CEO wished to communicate with me, I would offer him a specific time, one that would be the best use of his time and would allow me to arrive in good mental and physical condition. I would not casually say, "Let's get together some morning next week. I will give you a specific time at my convenience as it will depend on how busy my days are."

And I would block off all the time we both would need. During our time together, I would give the CEO a generous amount of time to share with me, and I would not do all the talking. That type of appointment would probably yield fruitful conversation. And that is what we should respectfully do for God.

Another technology that was far different in the '50s was television. Depending on where you lived, you might receive just 2 or 3 channels. In some geographic areas, the reception for one of those channels might not be very clear. You might have to add an enhancement to your antenna or move the antenna closer to the window. Similarly, in prayer, you must find the spot where your reception for hearing from Him is the best. Some prayer teachers insist that you must have a prayer room or, at least, a prayer closet. Some wonderful women of prayer I know do this and it is right for them. I have the room to have such a place, but my lifelong habit of praying by my bed is a familiar spot for the Lord and me. Dropping to my knees first thing in the morning is where He expects to meet me first. I move on later to my bed as I read His Word and pray as I go, being directed by whatever He is revealing to me in His Word. Maybe I like the intimacy of this habit that has worn a comfortable groove into my prayer life. Even though as an Army brat I changed schools six times in six years during my childhood, the unfailing way the Lord would meet me in whatever state or on whatever base we lived in was blessed assurance. It is how I saw my mother pray, and I know with absolute certainty she was a close and intimate friend of the Lord's; their communication was precious, and I had the privilege of watching it develop through the years. Saying prayers was the first thing I remember my mother teaching me, and in the final years of her life with Alzheimer's, it was something we shared till the very end. She no longer remembered even how to eat, but when I would read the passages she had marked in her Bible and pray for her aloud, an expression of such peace would settle over her face. Her entire demeanor would change. The Holy Spirit was still communicating with her in a way I will not understand on this earth, but may one day.

Like me, you have to find the place you can best have an extended visit with the Lord. At a minimum, it should be free of distraction. You may have to get up extra early to ensure that, as I did for the years I was a working single mom of a little one. It seems impossible at first. How can you give up that hour when your kids are small and you are so exhausted? But most people who try it are amazed at the rest they get and the change in their lives.

I am not being legalistic. Some people can carve out the time after the morning frenzy is over or some, I am told, in the evening. For many of us who tried that, we had to be honest that life would often intrude and we were unreliable about keeping that appointment with the Lord if we did not protect that time for communication first thing in the morning. And there is much precedent for praying in the mornings, including Jesus' practice of regularly setting aside alone time to talk with His Father *(And rising very early in the morning, while it was still dark, he departed and went out to a desolate place, and there he prayed. Mark 1:35.)* Or the example of the Godly man Job comes to mind *(And when the days of the feast had run their course, Job would send and consecrate them, and he would rise early in the morning and offer burnt offerings according to the number of them all Job 1:5.)* But the Lord will lead you to the right time and place if you ask Him because it aligns with His will.

And he said to him, "You shall love the Lord your God with all your heart and with all your soul and with all your mind. This is the great and first commandment." Matthew 22:37-40

Another thing about the 50s was that television, transistor radios, and landlines did not always get the crystal clear reception we have today, and there was static. Sometimes called interference, this distracting noise and sometimes snowy tv pictures resulted when you had two things going on at once. Your sister drying her hair in the next room could cause a line across the television screen or make an annoying noise if the two appliances were operating in parallel. Today, when you let phone calls and other distractions interrupt your time with Him, this can cause interference in your reception during prayer. Some people today say that they have their quiet time as they drive to work. I love praising the Lord and talking to him as I drive to work or on a long car trip, but that is a different type of communication than I have been referring to. When you do two things at once, you are not giving Him your full attention. Maybe you cannot give Him dedicated time every day, but He certainly deserves it. Finding time most days to give Him your undivided attention will bless you more than Him. That meeting with Him is first and foremost, and it can transform your career, your relationship with each family member, your friendship with Him, and most of all, the peace or lack of peace you live with. This old hymn says it best:

Turn your eyes upon Jesus,
Look full in His wonderful face,
And the things of earth will grow strangely dim,
  In the light of His glory and grace.

Helen H. Lemmel

I will conclude with the words of Paul, a man of great power through prayer and the Holy Spirit, a man who did not hesitate to ask for anything from the Father:

Let us then with confidence draw near to the throne of grace, that we may receive mercy and find grace to help in time of need. Hebrews 4:16

More Scripture to consider:

Psalm 88:13 *But I, O LORD, cry to you; in the morning my prayer comes before you.*

Psalm 119:147 *I rise before dawn and cry for help; I hope in your words.*

Psalm 5:3 *O LORD, in the morning you hear my voice; in the morning I prepare a sacrifice for you and watch.*

Proverbs 8:17 *I love those who love me, and those who seek me diligently find me.*

DEVOTIONAL 47: THANKSGIVING

It is a long story, but I am writing my Thanksgiving blog in mid-July because of a publishing deadline. I tried to wait until a bunch of wonderful things happened to me so I would be inspired to spontaneously give thanks and write a really upbeat blog. I wanted to be so bursting with thanksgiving that you would catch the overflow of my gratitude and the words would capture that type of joy when you just can't stop saying, "Thank you, Lord!" I wanted this blog to be about a series of love touches God was giving to me so we could share as believers that wonderful camaraderie of saying together, "Look what the Lord did for me!" July has not been that kind of month.

Rather, my focus has been on all that has gone wrong. When I looked at this week, I saw that my dear, longtime prayer partner is still in ICU, the young daughter of my closest neighbor friend died of cancer, one of the kindest, best people I know ran over a woman at a crosswalk and the woman died, and family rifts and divorces have erupted in the Godliest families I know. These are the people closest to me and I am grieving.

I go to the library every day to write because my AC has been out for a week, and I sleep on the sofa and conduct my business out of the library. Every day when I head to the library, I ask myself if this is a good day to write my Thanksgiving blog and my mind says, "No, wait until something good happens." Instead, more mishaps, financial, physical, and personal, just keep happening.

If you are a mature Christian, you probably know where this is headed. At some point yesterday, the Holy Spirit pulled me up short and shook me. He made me look, really look, at the reality of my life. He told me that this was the very day I should be writing my Thanksgiving blog because I am spectacularly blessed.

I am a child of God, the daughter of a King Who owns the cattle on a thousand hills. Every need I have has been met through all the recent trials, and they always will be. Psalm 37:25 says:

I have been young, and now am old,
  yet I have not seen the righteous forsaken
  or his children begging for bread.

I may go through lean times, but the Lord will not forsake me in them:

Keep your life free from love of money, and be content with what you have, for he has said, "I will never leave you nor forsake you." Hebrews 13:5

Not only is His eye on the sparrow but it never leaves me; He continually watches over me and cares for me:

29 Are not two sparrows sold for a penny?[i] And not one of them will fall to the ground apart from your Father. 30 But even the hairs of your head are all numbered. 31 Fear not, therefore; you are of more value than many sparrows. Matthew 10:29-31

I am loved extravagantly, so much so that my Father gave His only Son to die in my place, a death I richly deserved. The sinless, gentle Jesus lay down His life and paid for my pardon with His own blood. That reprieve alone is worthy of celebrating with Thanksgiving every day. The fact that Jesus came to earth expressly and willingly to lay down His life for me is something I should be saying, "Thank you, thank you, thank you" for every day without ceasing.

The more the Holy Spirit brought the reality to the forefront of my thoughts, the more my circumstances were put into perspective. These momentary and temporal difficulties receded far into the back landscape of my mind (2 Corinthians 4:17.) I know that I am supposed to lift my eyes above my circumstances, but I had been allowing them to consume my thoughts and conversations with others. I had the power of the Resurrection to talk about, the joy of my Salvation, and the love letter of Jesus' life, but all I had been talking about was the mundane. Forgive me, Lord! He told me exactly what to do to never fall into this pitiful state:

"You keep him in perfect peace whose mind is stayed on you, because he trusts in you." Isaiah 26:3

And He will keep my friends who trust in Him as well. Praise the Lord!

Though I know Him, though I love Him, and deep down I trust Him (so deep down no one could see it lately), my complaining indicated a weakness in that trust that was interrupting my peace. If I had meditated more on Him and spent more time in thanksgiving, I would have been filled with peace. I know He is trustworthy, but I was surely not a walking advertisement, especially to the many nonbelievers I was meeting in my trials.

I needed to be like Shadrach, Meshach, and Abednego, who were facing being thrown into a fiery furnace unlike any we know today. They were willing to walk into that fire because they trusted the Lord so completely. In Daniel 3:17, they say to their persecutor:

"If we are thrown into the blazing furnace, the God we serve is able to deliver us from it, and he will deliver us from Your Majesty's hand." NIV

Yes, they knew God might let them be thrown into that fire, but they had absolute assurance that their God was sovereign and that there would be a victory through Him in the end.

You may have had a year full of trials. You may feel you have been in the furnace. You may not see how a certain problem will be resolved. I urge you to start thanking Him for the victory that will ultimately be yours through Him. Call to remembrance every fiery trial He has brought you through in the past. Remember how surprising He is in the way he brings about deliverance.

More than anything this Thanksgiving, thank Him for the gift of your salvation that brings peace. Thank him that today's trials are momentary and that you will live a carefree, joyous life with Him in eternity after this short sojourn on earth. When you begin to fully focus on the thanksworthy gifts in your life, the momentary afflictions dwindle to earth size when juxtaposed to Heaven-size eternal blessings.

DEVOTIONAL 48: THANKFUL FOR THE LITTLE THINGS

In this current mode of thankfulness, I thought it might be fun to meditate on the little things God has done that make our lives so delightful. Yes, *"in this world we will have trouble,"* but we will also have moments when we take in His creation of breathtaking beauty that He formed for our mutual delight. We will have moments when we observe a lightning bug or a flock of geese with their unerring navigational skills or a drop of water under a microscope, and experience genuine awe. There has never been an architect who could fashion something as perfect and self-sustainable as a tree. There has never been an engineer who could invent a series of co-dependent systems that work as amazingly as the human body. There has never been a chemist who could create a solution that sustained life, maintained perfect Ph, hosted so many living creatures, and avoided stagnation and staved off pollution like the ocean. Each miracle is enough to keep me mesmerized for years if I truly wanted to try to figure out how He did it.

Let's not be complacent about the familiar miracles we take for granted. I mean, it really is an amazing thing to watch how a caterpillar builds a cocoon and emerges a butterfly. The stars across the black sky on a clear night are spectacular. Just because they have been there our entire lives, let's not forget to take in that light show that is free and better than any laser production I have ever paid for. And how do those little bird bodies fly so high and kick their babies out of the nest at just the perfect moment so they can fly as well? Oh, I know it is something about hollow bones, but God designed that anatomy so they could soar and enjoy just being a bird. It's their only job! Examine that rose closely, every part. No artist has an intricate, delicate design of so much beauty. Then look at a lily and a daisy and a hyacinth and see God's infinite creativity. Go stand at the bottom of a mountain if you can. Get a glimpse of God's magnitude.

Think of the last time someone noticed you—a kindness you did, something you did well, an insight you had. God gave them that glimpse and appreciation of you. Think of the last time you said something that warmed someone's heart or comforted a friend or made someone smile. God gave that observation or impulse to you. Think of your family or your church family or the family God has given you comprised of friends, past or present. Think of the family of our future we have to look forward to as we will live in perfect harmony together, sisters and brothers worshipping our Father all day long in Heaven.

This is the start of my list. What is on yours? What in humanity, nature, the Bible, God's character and creations has ever made you grateful? Praise Him for those today.

DEVOTIONAL 49: THE MANGER OF MY HEART

Dear friends, I am sharing with you a Christmas carol I wrote many years ago when my heart was cold to anything that resembled the Christmas spirit. I was a busy single mom, and I just had nothing but a bare heart to offer Him, so I came to Him in the honesty of the words below.

The night is dark

And we're alone,

Not a sound stirs the night air.

I have finally settled down

And put down daily cares.

I've bustled through my week at work,

And made sure shopping's done.

The only person I've overlooked

Is God's own Holy Son.

CHORUS

Welcome to the manger of my heart.

Welcome to the manger of my heart.

It's not much to offer you,

But you can change it through and through.

Come, Sweet Jesus, make it new, and

Welcome to the manger of my heart.

The manger where you lay, my Lord,

When you became the Living Word

Didn't look so good at first.

It had its rough spots, it'd been misused,

And if you want to know the truth,

My heart's that way and dark as soot.

But if God can choose a manger

For the crib of a King,

Then I know He can take my heart

And do most anything.

CHORUS

So I kneel here in the darkness,

And I offer my heart to you.

If a miracle's going to happen, Lord,

It's got to be up to you.

I'm just here on my knees,

And I don't know where to start,

Except to say, I love you, Lord, and

Welcome to the manger of my heart.

CHORUS

I heard a preacher say long ago,

And I really hope it's so,

That all it takes to begin again

Is to say "Please, Jesus, enter in,

 and I'm really sorry about all the sin."

So if it's that easy to make a new start,

Then I'm coming to you to do my part,

Oh, Lord come down and change me today,

Come on, Lord, I pray…

And welcome to the manger of my heart.

CHORUS

DEVOTIONAL 50: THE DARK EDGE OF SIN VERSUS THE LIGHT OF GRACE

You can only experience life's greatest joy by first looking at its darkest stain- sin. In the midst of the sin message you will find the Grace message. You will find the Resurrection message. You will find the salvation message. You will find the Christmas message.

In the middle of the beautiful retelling of Christ's birth in Matthew 1:21, you will find the angel saying this about Mary:

*"She will bear a son, and you shall call his name Jesus, for he will save his people **from their sins**."*

That is why He came to earth. The whole reason. Sin necessitated it. His love wiped the sin away. The darkness of sin is repugnant, but it makes the undeserved forgiveness so glorious, generous, and undeserved.

When John the Baptist sees Jesus approaching him for baptism, he says, *"Look, the Lamb of God, who takes away the sin of the world!"* This is the first and foremost identity John the Forerunner of Christ ascribes to Jesus—that He will *"take away the sin of the world."* Not make excuses for your sin and mine. Not get a reduced sentence. Take it away!

When I sin, I at first feel stuck, especially if it is a sin that I have battled before and thought I would never do again. Some people call these our pet sins, ones we are very familiar with and may even view as secondary to other sins. Not so. Sin is sin.

When I commit a sin, I am tempted to stay mired in regret and self-contempt. The enemy tries to fasten my eyes on my guilt to the point that I cannot move forward in praise or service, but that is not what Christ would have me do. In the moment of my greatest despair that I have once again sinned, a voice comes into my heart and says, "This is what the Cross was for! This is why I came. Do you think my blood is not effective enough for this sin? If not for this, then what?" Then relief floods my heart, and I have a moment of great gratitude all over again that He willingly died and paid the price, rose again, and

CONQUERED ALL SIN! CONQUERED _MY_ SIN! This is what the Cross was for! This is what the Advent was for!

The only way to completely escape sin is through the Lord. This petition from _Psalm 19:13_ also asks for God's help:

13 _Keep back your servant also from presumptuous sins; let them not have dominion over me! Then I shall be blameless, and innocent of great transgression._

And _I John 1:7_ gives us this encouragement about the results of facing our sin, confessing our sin, and turning away from our sin:

7 _But if we walk in the light, as he is in the light, we have fellowship with one another, and the blood of Jesus his Son cleanses us from all sin._

John 16:33 affirms that sin has already been defeated by our Lord:

33 _I have said these things to you, that in me you may have peace. In the world you will have tribulation. But take heart; I have overcome the world. John 16:33._

I look forward to the day when I will no longer be here on earth where sin prowls around trying to engage me and tempt me to react in ways that are not in sync with the character of Jesus, whom I long to emulate. I pray for you and for me that we will turn to Him faster and not linger over the temptation to have our own way and do what we may feel justified to do. His approach to treating others is not at all the world's way. I pray for you and me that we will every day react more in the Lord's way than in the world's way. Only Christ can cleanse sin, but He tells us to "Resist!"

 Submit yourselves therefore to God. Resist the devil, and he will flee from you.

James 4:7

DEVOTIONAL 51: NEW YEAR: JUDGMENT VERSUS INDIFFERENCE

I attended a Bible study on Tuesday nights last summer taught by some young women who challenged me and taught me and inspired my walk. We were assigned a table of women to go through the study with, and my table has been authentic and loving toward one another since the first night we met. We were sharing prayer requests recently, and I shared that I desired God's help with what I observe. With all the beautiful, amazing things God is doing all around me every day, I can sometimes notice the unlovely more. Last week, I was with another group of women and someone made a negative remark; then two other women commented in agreement *(We have all been guilty of that, right?)* The remarks took a gathering that had been marked by unity and adoration of Christ in a different direction. I went beyond not joining in the critical words of others to being critical myself of those who did join in. I wish I had not noticed. I wish I had been so focused on the dozen sweet and exciting things that were happening in that room and had let what was said just not even register in my memory. My favorite version of this command is the King James Version:

Finally, brethren, whatsoever things are true, whatsoever things are honest, whatsoever things are just, whatsoever things are pure, whatsoever things are lovely, whatsoever things are of good report; if there be any virtue, and if there be any praise, think on these things. Philippians 4:8

I was allowing my mind to think on the unlovely.

The morning after I had asked my Tuesday group to pray for me, my daily Bible reading included Psalm 12. That chapter comes out strongly against words from the double-hearted, speaking words of vanity with your neighbor, and errors of the lips. I questioned the Lord on this and was wondering if perhaps I had not been wrong to react to the critical words I had heard. After praying and thinking about this more, here are some conclusions I have drawn:

1. Isaiah 5:20a says, *"Woe to those who call evil good and good evil."* So I would have been wrong to condone what I

heard. It was not wrong of me to have noticed something that was Biblically out of order.

2. The tricky part comes with what we do with an observation like that once we see it. There are definitely times we are to go to our sisters (after MUCH prayer) and say, "I know your heart and that you seek the Lord. I want you to tell me when (not if) I say anything that does not reflect Christ or my walk, and I hope you will want me to tell you the same, because I love you and I admire your walk. I want us to be iron sharpening iron in each other's lives *(Proverbs 27:17.)* Because of that, I felt what you said yesterday contradicted Verse X. Let's pray about it and see what the Lord tells us. And let's talk about it when it is convenient for you." There is a very good chance the Lord has already convicted her of the problem. There is also a good chance that you will not receive the response you desire. That is okay. If, and only if, God prompts you to go the person in love and speak the truth, you must do it. You both will grow from it.

> *Rather, speaking the truth in love, we are to grow up in every way into him who is the head, into Christ. Ephesians 4:15*

3. At times, however, the Lord has told me that my opinion or approval or disapproval of what was said is unwanted and unnecessary. It is not my job to convict or to even weigh in when the issue is between the Holy Spirit and the other person. Knowing the difference between these situations and the one described above in #2 requires much prayer. Being a teacher for forty-five years makes it too easy for me to be "instructive." Ecclesiastes 3:7-8 says there is *"a time to tear and a time to sew; a time to be silent and a time to speak; a time to love and a time to hate; a time for war and a time for peace."*

4. Whether I mentioned what was said to the people involved was not the issue. My heart was the issue. I came to believe the Lord was convicting me of pride and judgmentalism. Dwelling on the sin of others is a misappropriation of my time when I have plenty of my own sin I could be talking to the Lord about.

And He is well capable of getting their attention through the amazing work of the Holy Spirit. Though it was not a sin to know the Bible well enough to know that what was said was a sin, it was a conversation between the Lord and them that was needed. In other words, it was none of my business in this case.

5. Finally, the Lord showed me a sort of continuum related to guilt and conviction of sin. This continuum shows a range of how people look (or don't look) at their sin. It ranges from people who dwell too much on looking backward at forgiven sin and may have false guilt to the other end of the spectrum of people who do not acknowledge sin. The continuum looks like this:

Do not acknowledge many sins	Need to be listening to the Holy Spirit more; not highly aware of own sin	PERFECT	Take time away from worship & service thinking about sins God already forgave	False guilt; Legalism; Self-abnegation

Because one of satan's ploys in my life is to cause me to dwell on my actions and stir up false guilt, I at first thought that perhaps I was not wrong in the case of my reaction to the words of the women in the meeting.   But after some prayer, I realized that I felt the conviction of the Holy Spirit over my own sin. Though I had not repeated what happened or criticized the women, I had wasted valuable time and energy telling myself how regrettable *their* remarks were. That was not my place this time.   Also, I could feel my very fleshly response, and it was not Christlike. By now, unfortunately, I know what it feels like to have my flesh rise up and distract me from being led wholly by Him.

It is a wonderful thing for God to reveal your sin to you. It is the beginning of freedom from the hold that particular sin has on you. It is a wonderful thing to know that you are not responsible to convict others. Yes, we speak the truth in love when our hearts are pure and the Lord leads us that way, but we do not need to weigh in on social media or in conversations on everyone else's sin.

Why do I post this blog so close to New Year's? Because this is a sin I want to pray about and ask God to rid me of in the coming year. I want to grow stronger in resisting the temptation of observing the behavior of others more than observing my own wayward heart. I want to entrust my brothers and sisters more to the Lord. I want to be so busy engaging with Him as he deals with me on my sin that I do not look sideways at anyone else's, unless I am responsible as a family member or in some other role to deal with the sin.

If you decide to use the continuum above to examine your own sin, keep this one thing in mind:

We can be very sensitive to some kinds of sins such as lying or adultery, even to the point of having false guilt; yet we might have another type of sin such as gossip or excess that we have become insensitive to. Consider that as you try to decide where you fall on the spectrum.

Other verses about keeping silent:

Ephesians 4:26 Be angry and do not sin; do not let the sun go down on the cause of your anger.

Proverbs 10:19 Transgression is at work where people talk too much, but anyone who holds his tongue is prudent.

Proverbs 21:23 Whoever guards his mouth and his tongue keeps himself out of trouble.

DEVOTIONAL 52: WHAT DID YOUR FATHER GIVE YOU FOR CHRISTMAS?

Because He is a good Father, all of His gifts are good, starting with the amazing, life-changing gift of our salvation. In this season when we are so aware of earthly gifts, I want to pause for a moment to think about one of the many gifts our Father blesses us with and wants us to receive fully. I have mentioned this next gift I love before, but I have saved this one last thing of what He has revealed to me for us to unwrap at Christmas—about the gift of The Wide Place. This gift will bring you the comfort and joy that the hymns and carols speak of. It will bring you relief from stress that most of us so badly need, especially at this time of year. The Wide Place offers you a large and roomy space to run freely in Him, a spot in your journey where your feet won't stumble, and liberty like you have never known.

What does The Wide Place have to do with Christmas? Psalm 18:19 speaks of our salvation as a rescue; *"He brought me into a spacious place, he rescued me because he delighted in me."* The story of Christ's coming is the story of the greatest rescue mission the world has ever known. Popular movies show rescue missions for a few or maybe scores of people, but Christ's mission to come to earth to rescue you and me extends to millions of people throughout many centuries. According to Psalm 18:19, The Wide Place is a spacious place where God brings us for rest and restoration. Are you needing that right now?

At the beginning of the story in Matthew 1:20-21, we find Joseph, who has just learned that Mary, his betrothed, is with child. The troubling and undoubtedly heartbreaking issue is that they have never been together intimately. Joseph determines to end the relationship quietly, but God has a different plan. An angel appears to Joseph and says:

20 But after he had considered this, an angel of the Lord appeared to him in a dream and said, "Joseph son of David, do not be afraid to take Mary home as your wife, because what is conceived in her is from the Holy Spirit. 21 She will give birth to a son, and you are to give him the name Jesus, because he will save his people from their sins.

185

This root word for Jesus in this passage is "yasha," meaning "God will save," according to Dr. John E. Hartley in his *Theological Wordbook of the Old Testament*. Vol 1, pp. 414-15. But this word can also mean "to make wide."

So Jesus came to save and to give us a wide and roomy path through His sacrifice, because He knew we could not walk this path of life unless He did the hard work for us. Without Him, we would stumble and never get up. He knew when He came to earth as a baby that He was coming to rescue us from our sins. But He also intended to continue to walk with us and make a Wide Place for us through His love and mercy.

Proverbs 4:12 says He even places our feet on a path, and it is a path that will aid us in not stumbling:

When you walk, your step will not be hampered, and if you run, you will not stumble.

According to the ASV version of Psalm 18:36, the Lord will actually enlarge the path under your feet to keep you from stumbling:

Thou hast enlarged my steps under me, And my feet have not slipped.

The fact that Jesus was coming to place us in The Wide Place was announced centuries before in Isaiah 61:1:

The Spirit of the Lord GOD is upon me,
 because the LORD has anointed me
to bring good news to the poor;
 he has sent me to bind up the brokenhearted,
to proclaim liberty to the captives,
 and the opening of the prison to those who are bound;

This verse again tells us that God does not just save us as a one-time "experience." He walks beside us for the rest of our lives, binding up our broken hearts and freeing us from whatever is holding us captive. My favorite part of this verse is Jesus' mission *"to proclaim liberty to the captives."* My sin can sometimes hold me captive until I release whatever thoughts or hurts or outlooks to Him. What has held your heart captive lately that Jesus can deliver you from?

If you haven't had a Christmas get-together with the Lord this season, now may be a good time. Thank Him for the gift of your salvation, but thank Him that He continues to guide your feet and will walk with you in The Wide Place until we see Him face-to-face.

Ask the Lord to take you into the new year with your heart firmly planted in Him and, if it is His perfect timing, your feet set down in The Wide Place. Enter the new year with a grateful heart and a reliance on Him to guide your every step.

DEEPER STILL_____OPTIONAL
QUESTIONS FOR STUDY & REFLECTION

Series: Stones of Remembrance

Devotionals 1-3

1. This is a week to reflect on all God has been saying through the stories of Joshua, Jacob, and others. What other ways do people in the Bible acknowledge God, His power, and his sovereignty? You don't have to limit yourself to Hannah, Abraham, David, or Mary, but these people certainly are examples to consider.

2. Jacob set up his pillar *after* he had received the blessing from the Lord. Do you pray more before you receive a blessing or deliverance from trouble or after? What in your life can you use to bring Him glory—words, resources, gifts, music, etc.?

3. Devotional 2's lesson says, "Giving the Lord His due always comes first. He is not to fit around our list of priorities, our schedules, and our waxing and waning energy levels. He comes first." Do you see these statements being played out clearly for *others* to see in your life? If not, what will you do or say to make honoring Him a higher priority on your to-do list?

4. In Devotional 2's lesson, the Lord also tells Joshua: "When your children ask in time to come, 'What do those stones mean to you?' **7** then you shall tell them that the waters of the Jordan were cut off before the ark of the covenant of the Lord." So stones of remembrance may not just be for our private acknowledgment of the Lord, but He may use what you say or do in the lives of others.

Are there children in your life who see you acknowledging God for all He has done for you? If there are not children, might there be a neighbor, acquaintance, or co-worker who could be watching and listening if you were to make a beautiful acknowledgment of Him?

5.   Read 1 Kings 5-9. What is the difference between Adonijah and the characters we have studied who set up stones of remembrance? How might a person today pay tribute to himself or herself?

6.   I would love to hear your thoughts about stones of remembrance. Was there a Biblical person who inspired you?

7. Have you ever done something to acknowledge God for His mercy, character, or provision?

Series: Lord, I Am Willing

Devotionals 4-7

8. Is there something the Lord wants you to be more willing to do? It may be just an area of your life and or in your walk with Him that could be stronger.

9. What might be some of your barriers to being willing to go and do anything the Holy Spirit brings to your mind? Comfort? Family? Finances? Other?

10. What other people in the Bible demonstrate a willingness to say, "Lord I am willing?"

11. Do you serve God more from a sense of duty or do you serve Him as a response to His outpouring of love for you? Describe how you feel about God's extravagant love for you as described in Devotional 7.

12. Have you ever prioritized or valued another kind of love over God's love? How might this be reflected in your life now or in the past?

Series: Conquering Sinful Responses such as Judgmentalism and Self-centeredness

Devotionals 8-10

13. Look over Devotional 8, and the eight things women take from good to bad. Which might be an area where you could be vulnerable to take a bit too far?

14. Have you ever been gobsmacked by a sermon, remark, or a verse as described in Devotional 9?

15. Can you think of anyone who brings out the judgmental side of you and prompts you to evaluate what they are doing in small or big ways? What do you think God wants you to do in regard to that person?

16. Reviewing Devotional 10, what would you be willing to sacrifice to have greater intimacy with God? Is there a situation where you are pushing to be right or for your rights? Pray and ask if God is asking you to let that go and trust Him to take care of your needs.

Series: Fellow sinners: The Woman at the Well and Reuben

Devotionals 11-13

17. Do you see Reuben more as a valiant leader or as a sinner? Explain your answer.

18. Do you in any way relate to Reuben? In what ways?

19. We see four Grace points in Reuben's life. Are you aware of a time God has shown you Grace (unmerited favor)?

20. Devotional 13 says we should "walk a wide circle around choices, situations, places, and events that can damage our witness to the unsaved and those younger or weaker in their walks." Are there neighbors, co-workers, nephews, or other family members who might be aware of your Christian walk? Is there anything in your life that could make your testimony less honoring to the Lord?

Series: Prayer and Preparing Your Heart for Easter and Spring

Devotionals 14-16

21. Have you ever gone through a time when your prayers seemed barren or unanswered? What did you do? What might you do after reading Devotional 14?

22. Five reasons are given for confession and repentance (Devotional 15.) Which of the five reasons motivates you most to confess and repent this Easter season?

23. Read the Scriptures in Devotionals 14-16. Which will be most valuable to you to memorize or reread this week?

Series: The God of Yes: Compassion on Earth and Joy in Heaven

Devotionals 17-19

24. For most of your life, have you viewed God as the God of "yes" or "no?" Why? What does the Bible say?

25. When you think of death and Heaven, are your thoughts similar to the ones in Devotional 18? How are your thoughts different?

26. People who do not believe in our Lord often question how God can allow death, fear, and suffering. Is there anything in Devotional 19 you might use to address these concerns?

Series: Women in Jesus' Life

Devotionals 20-27. *Includes these special devotionals:*

22- Memorial Day: Why Christians Honor Veterans and Fallen Soldiers

24- The Heart Cry of God – A Father's Day Message

25- How Does God Feel about You?

27. Is there a dark or difficult place where God has placed you now or in the past where you could shine and be a living example of a Christlike response?

28. What women in your sphere do you admire who humbly serve the Lord and may not get the recognition that teachers or leaders receive?

29. In addition to the women mentioned in Devotionals 20-27, what other Biblical women do you admire?

30. Based on Devotional 22, summarize why Christians should honor veterans.

31. Jesus respected authority. What people of authority or types of authority are difficult for you to respect? Could Jesus have made similar excuses if He wanted to?

32. In the Mary and Martha story, what are Mary's strengths? Which gift was probably not Mary's strong suit **(1 Corinthians 12: 8–10, 1 Peter 4:9–10)?**

33. What are Martha's strengths? Weaknesses?

34. What do you learn from the life of Mary Magdalene?

35. Have you ever read about the life of Absalom and his relationship with his father David? How does their relationship compare to our relationship with God?

36. Devotional 25 asks, "How Does God Feel about You?" Based on Scriptures in this devotional or elsewhere, summarize how you would answer that question.

Series: Being Under Attack Is Followed by Entering the Wide Place

Devotionals 28-31

37. When you are under attack, what verses in Devotional 28 encourage you? Look in the paragraphs and at the end. What verses would you add to encourage others?

38. How did Jesus respond to satan's attacks?

39. Why do you think Jesus said the following to Peter?

"18 And I tell you that you are Peter, and on this rock I will build my church, and the gates of Hades will not overcome it. 19 I will give you the keys of the kingdom of heaven; whatever you bind on earth will be bound in heaven, and whatever you loose on earth will be loosed in heaven."

How did Peter do during his night of testing? What does this say to you about your life and your sin?

40. Think about your life since you became a Christian. Have you ever been in The Wide Place?

41. When you personally have experienced being in a broad and spacious place or time with the Lord, have you told others about it to encourage them? Why or why not?

42. What form does your personal worship times with Him take? Do you sing, play music, write poems, tell Him what you love about His wonderful attributes?

43. Please read all Scriptures in Devotional 40. What is your greatest takeaway about worshipping Him?

Series: Guest Bloggers

Devotionals 32-36

Includes a special Labor Day Blog

44. Do you have difficulty being still before the Lord? What do you do to prepare to be still?

45. In Devotional 33, what was the meaning of the analogy about the cookies?

46. Have you ever felt God was holding out on you or holding something back that you badly wanted?   Describe that experience and any results or fruit that followed.

47. Devotional 34 on prayer asks you "how personal God is to you when praying? Personal enough to Chat with? Walk with? Laugh with? Be silent with? Listen to? Sing to?"

Which of those responses would you like to strengthen during your prayer time?

48. Devotional 34 also asks if your "fellowshipping with Jesus is not so personal, but mainly …
Asking forgiveness? Quoting Scriptures? Giving praise? Doing most of the talking?"

On average, how would you say your prayer time is allocated among those items? You may add items of your own. Example: Asking forgiveness-5% / Quoting Scriptures-10% / Giving praise-15% / Doing most of the talking-60% / Listening-5% / Other-5%."

49. Devotional 35 asks you to look at something in your life that is very important to you. What would you choose to examine in your own life with Leslie Harder's question: "If God is not first in my (fill in the blank), then God is not first in my life." Example: "If God is not first in my relationship with my child, then God is not first in my life."

50. If you have experienced grief, would you say you built a road or a wall in response to the loss (Devotional 35)? If you have never experienced grief, what future grief might God be preparing you for? Losses are not always the death of someone but of a dream, a profession, etc.

51. If you were the only Christian that people in your workplace ever saw in their lives, what would be your co-worker's description of what behaviors a Christian displays? What would your boss say your behavior says about Christians? What about people who report to you, customers, neighbors, and others?

52. Which verses in Devotional 36 will help you witness through your work going forward?

Series: The Mind of Christ and the Humor of God

Devotionals 37-38

53. Explain in your own words what taking on the mind of Christ means?

54. Do you believe God has a sense of humor? Why or why not?

55. Devotional 38 says: "Another thing I learned is that it really depends on what is in your heart whether your laughter is good or bad, wise or foolish. For example, when Sarah first overheard she was going to have a baby in her old age, she laughed in disbelief or at least underestimation of what God can do."

Where have you experienced the wrong kind of laughter about God, either in our own life or from being around others? What do people need who laugh in the wrong way about God?

Series: True Friendship

Devotionals 39-40

56. What role can a Christian friend play in the life of friend to strengthen her? Describe how you do this for your friend(s). Is there someone new the Lord may be leading you to befriend to strengthen her walk?

57. What Biblical basis is there for believing God wants us to have Godly friendships?

Series: Arming Yourself to Face the World with Prayer, Worship, and Blessing Your Enemy

Devotionals 41-43

58. Which of the role models described in Devotional 41 could be helpful for you to think about and perhaps learn from? Do you disagree with any of them?

59. For one week, experiment with one of the strategies the women in Devotional 41 uses to fight off sin. Try to be dead to offense and your own self-interest as Julie Van Gorp suggests. Or try to put on the full armor of God every morning in a very thoughtful and intentional way as Ann Kieffer suggests. How did it affect your week?

60. What would you add to a week of adoration? What verses would you recite? What songs would you sing? What would you do during such a week?

61. Devotional 43 suggests we are to go beyond simple forgiveness and serve our enemy the way David served Saul. After reading this devotional, do you think God has ever asked you to play your lyre for your enemy? Who in your life now might He be asking you to serve and bless?

62. What Biblical motivation might you have to play your lyre for your enemy after reading this devotional or as the Lord leads you?

Series: Where the Power Lies: In Trust, Communication, and Not in Self

Devotionals 44-46

63. When was Uzziah strong? Why did he become weak?

64. What lesson can you learn from Uzziah and how can you apply it to your life?

65. Why do we need not to be careful (in the sense of "full of care")? What Scriptures support that statement?

66. What do you need to change in your life to keep your channels even clearer?

Series: Thanksgiving, Christmas, and New Year's

Devotionals 47-52

67. Which of the Scriptures in Devotional 47 prompts you to be thankful?

68. Devotional 48 mentions the everyday miracle of the stars against the backdrop of the dramatic night sky. Which other everyday miracles might we be taking for granted and not taking time to notice and thank God for?

69. Devotionals 47 and 48 mention reasons to be thankful. Which of those, if any, are you most likely to take for granted? What other things has the Lord done for you that you have not acknowledged lately? Devotional 48 says: "Think of the last time someone noticed you—a kindness you did, something you did well, an insight you had." What did you think of?

Now what can you tell God that you noticed that **He** did?

70. How is your heart like a manger?

71. Why is Devotional 50 about the "dark edge of sin" included as a Christmas devotional?

72. After reading the Scriptures in Devotionals 50-51, what can you do about sin?

73. When did the author's sin begin, as described in Devotional 51?

74. Explain this statement from Devotional 51: "It is a wonderful thing for God to reveal your sin to you."

75. Devotional 51 quotes Philippians 4:8:

Finally, brethren, whatsoever things are true, whatsoever things are honest, whatsoever things are just, whatsoever things are pure, whatsoever things are lovely, whatsoever things are of good report; if there be any virtue, and if there be any praise, think on these things. Philippians 4:8

What do you do very purposefully to think on good things and avoid thinking on unlovely things or impure things?

76. Devotional 51 has a scale or a continuum that runs 1-10. It is not good to be on the extreme of either end of the scale- a 1 or a 10. We strive to have balance between the two. Which end of the spectrum do you tend to be nearer—the low end or the high end? What can you do to be closer to the center?

1........2.........3..............4..............5..............6.........7.........8.........9........10				
Do not acknowledge many sins	Need to be listening to the Holy Spirit more; not highly aware of own sin	PERFECT	Take time away from worship & service thinking about sins God already forgave	False guilt; Legalism; Self-abnegation

77. We explored The Wide Place earlier this year. What new aspects of The Wide Place are added in Devotional 52? Why is this devotional included for New Year's?

78. Why does God bring us into The Wide Place?

79. According to Devotional 52, how can we keep from stumbling?

80. Thousands of years ago, a prophet announced some of Christ's reasons for leaving Heaven and coming to earth:

The Spirit of the Lord GOD is upon me,
*   because the LORD has anointed me*
to bring good news to the poor;
*   he has sent me to bind up the brokenhearted,*

to proclaim liberty to the captives,
    and the opening of the prison to those who are bound;
Isaiah 61:1

Which phrase or purpose for Christ's coming in the lines above do you need most right now and for the upcoming year? He gave up Heaven and accepted the cross in order to do these things for you, and you can be sure of that. Have a Happy New Year in the power of that!

How Did This Book Come to Be?

52 WEEKLY DEVOTIONALS FROM EVERYDAY TRUTH: ONCE A WEEK, GO DEEPER WITH GOD is a collection of blogs from the site AdventuresinChristianity.net. Casey Hawley has written these blogs that appeal to both the heart and the mind. Casey began to see how the Holy Spirit was blessing blog subscribers and how they were sending them to believers and non-believers alike. Then in the spring of 2019, four people contacted Casey **in one week** to say they believed the blogs were meant to be published in book form. Though not the original intention of the blogs, Casey prayerfully considered it.

Casey's first book, *Adventures in Christianity*, had been blessed to be used by the Lord to draw believers into greater trust and relationship with the Lord, and had also been used as an introduction to salvation for some. Some original readers of that book often buy five or six copies at a time to take to unsaved relatives, to share with co-workers, or to enrich the faith of the marginal believers in their lives. After prayer and consideration of how God had used the first book, Casey felt that the Lord was leading her to collect these devotionals into the book you hold now. May God bless you as you read it.

52 WEEKLY DEVOTIONALS FROM

EVERYDAY TRUTH

ONCE A WEEK, GO DEEPER WITH GOD

Do you really want to know God better? Once a week, immerse yourself in an enjoyable devotional that will deepen your relationship with Him. This book offers 52 conversation starters for weekly appointments with God you will not want to miss. God wants to do a new thing in your life. Use this book to refresh your love for Him. These Bible-based, sound readings reverence the Word of God but are filled with humor and joy.

What if you are not a Christian?

This is the perfect time for you to read this particular book. Consider this: What if there really is a God with a capital "G"? Shouldn't you want to be introduced to Him? Even some Christians have faulty views of God and His identity. **52 WEEKLY DEVOTIONALS FROM EVERYDAY TRUTH: ONCE A WEEK, GO DEEPER WITH GOD** is full of truth and will give you a foundation that is accurate. It will tell you all you need to know about the one true God who set the universe in motion and created the world from nothingness—including you!

EVERYDAY TRUTH

Author

Casey Hawley is a Christian author and speaker, a Bible teacher, and an encourager and teacher of women. She serves in prayer and in service to younger women at her church, Church of the Apostles in Atlanta. Casey has written and consulted on materials for several national ministries. Inquiries can be submitted to ChristianityAdventures@gmail.com

Casey published six successful business books before devoting herself to Christian writing and speaking. She has consulted with Fortune 500 companies on business writing for thirty years and previously taught in the business school at Georgia State University until 2017.

Made in the USA
Columbia, SC
18 November 2019